Ordnance Su...
The
Peak District
Landranger Guidebook

JARROLD

How to use this Guide

Pre-planning:
First look at the KEY MAP section — this shows the area covered, the towns and villages, and the starting point for the 12 Walks and 10 Tours. If you are unfamiliar with the area, look up some of the towns and villages in the PLACES OF INTEREST section. The WALKS or TOURS will provide further local information. The introductions will give you a feeling for the history, landscape, and wildlife of the area.

On the Spot:
From your chosen base, explore the area by road or on foot. Stars (★) after a place name indicate that it is featured in the PLACES OF INTEREST section (this is necessary as it is not possible to include every village and town because of space limitations). Some 28 places of interest are accompanied by maps to enable you to plan a short stroll. The scale of these is 2½ INCHES to 1 MILE (see CONVENTIONAL SIGNS for rights of way etc).

Landranger Maps:
These are the natural companions to the Guide. Places of interest are identified first with the number of the Landranger Map on which it appears (sometimes more than one). This is followed by two letters indicating the National Grid Square and by a 4-figure reference number. To locate any place or feature referred to on the relevant Landranger map, first read the two figures along the north or south edges of the map, then the two figures along the east or west edges. Trace the lines adjacent to each of the two sets of figures across the map face, and the point where they intersect will be the south-west corner of the grid square in which the place or feature lies.

Acknowledgements

We should like to thank those individuals and organisations who helped in the compilation of this book: Jill Brown and David Skelhon who chose the walks and tours, suggested the photographic selection, and compiled and wrote the text; Roland Smith and Harry Jones of the Peak District National Park; the helpful staff of the Peak Park Information Centres, the Tourist Information Centres, the Peak District Mining Museum, the Glossop Heritage Centre and Information Centre and the Wirksworth Heritage Centre; Neil Curtis for the index; Richard Garratt for the captioning; Paula Chasty for the artwork; Curtis Garratt Limited for editing, designing, and typesetting the guide.

First published 1990 by Ordnance Survey and Jarrold Colour Publications

Ordnance Survey
Romsey Road
Maybush
Southampton SO9 4DH

Jarrold Colour
Publications
Barrack Street
Norwich NR3 1TR

Printed in Great Britain by Jarrold and Sons Ltd. Norwich

Contents

KEY MAP INDEX

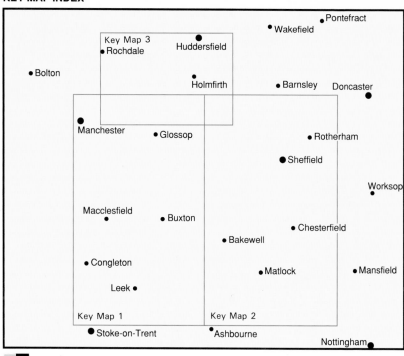

Image	Label
🚗 **4**	Motor and Cycle Tour Start
✏ **6**	Walk Start
✏	Mini-Walk Start

LANDRANGER MAPS OF THE PEAK DISTRICT

Key Map 1

SCALE 1:250 000 or 4 MILES to 1 INCH

0 1 km = 0·6214 mile   5   10   Kilometres 15

0 1 mile = 1·61 kms   5   Miles   10

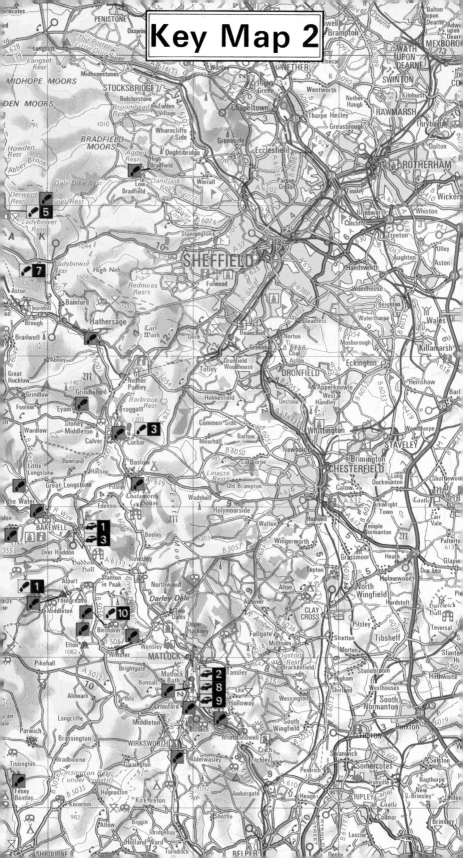

Key Map 2

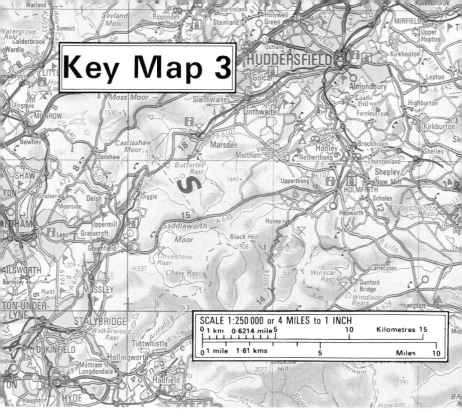

Key Map 3

SCALE 1:250 000 or 4 MILES to 1 INCH

Peter's Stone, Cressbrook Dale.

7

Introduction
The Peak District

Visit the Peak District on any summer Sunday and it is not hard to believe that it is one of the most visited National Parks in the world. The reason for this popularity is easy to establish as the outstandingly beautiful countryside that fully fills its 542 square miles. This is almost an insignificant area when compared with the vast National Parks of North America, but crammed into its confining boundaries is scenery of exceptional quality and surprising diversity. Indeed, it is because of this diversity that the Park appeals to such numbers and variety of people who drive over, walk on, climb up, or crawl under the Peakland landscape. They all come for seemingly different reasons — the motorist may visit a stately home, the walker may seek the solitude of the moors, the climber may wish to conquer a gritstone edge, and the caver investigate the challenge of the unlit depths — but they all in their way acknowledge the unique and precious collection of resources in the Peak.

It is a particularly important landscape because of its position at the boundary between the gentler, cultivated scenery of southern and eastern Britain and the harsher, wilder country of the north and west. Approaching from the south, the countryside undergoes a sharp metamorphosis from hedgerows, cornfields and villages of brick to bleached and skeletal limestone walls, grassy pasture and stone

Left: The well-worn path of the Pennine Way at Kinder Low. Below: Climbers on The Roaches.

cottages. The people talk 'funny', in a blunt, economising dialect that reflects their habitat and lifestyle. This nodal location at the crossroads of two contrasting landscapes — and, dare it be said, cultures — draws many people who wish to experience something more elemental than could possibly be found amidst the concrete and asphalt of the cities. Part of the appeal of the Peak District is its resistance to neat stereotyping. Travelling even short distances across the National Park, it soon becomes apparent that, although it has been clearly delineated and neatly parcelled up within its official boundaries, it is impossible to draw up a description of a 'typical' Peakland landscape.

A particular attraction of the Peak is the opportunity to choose which type of setting best suits the mood, personal capabilities, or weather conditions of the day. The choice is considerable and each visitor has his or her favourites. The serious walker may well prefer the austere solitude of the high plateaus, among the peat and heather with just sheep and curlew for company. Some may prefer the warm rocks of the south-west with their craggy outlines and panoramic views over the plain to the south, and still others may wish to gaze from the top of some artistically weathered tor along a gritstone escarpment. Many visitors, though, find the emerald pastures and cosier villages of the limestone plateaus more inviting, and if the wind is blowing hard, it is possible to seek shelter amidst the stunning beauty of the dales. Dovedale is world renowned and there have probably been many visitors who would agree with John Ruskin's observation that: 'The whole gift of the country is in its glens.'

The foundations of the land

The countryside, of course, reflects the nature of its physical foundations, and the explanation for this wonderful variety of landscape lies largely with the underlying rocks. In the Peak District these are of three main types which have been laid down in layers on top of one another. The oldest rock at the bottom is the limestone, deposited some 360-325 million years ago, and which is now exposed as the White Peak. In the middle are the softer shales — a kind of flaky, hardened mud often occupied by river valleys — and on top is the coarse, dark grit that forms the moorland and 'Edges' of the Dark Peak. Around 280 million years ago these strata were inten-sively folded and pushed up into a great dome that could have reached a maximum of 10,000 feet at its highest central point. Subsequent erosion then levelled off the landscape removing the topmost layers of grit and shale to reveal the limestone underneath. This has left the broad pattern of rocks we see today with a central oval-shaped core of limestone surrounded by a horseshoe of shales and millstone grit.

Although many people associate the Peak with the limestone, it does in fact form only about 1/4 of the Park. It occurs as a slightly tilted plateau rising to over 1500 feet in the north but struggling to reach 1200 feet in the south. The Dark Peak is

A peculiar rock

All limestones are easily dissolved by rainfall which turns into weak carbonic acid by absorbing carbon dioxide from the atmosphere. This dissolves the limestone and, in conjunction with the jointed nature of the rock, has led to some unusual features in the landscape — both above and below the ground! It may seem odd at first that the high land of the White Peak should seem so lacking in water, especially with the presence of so many 'dry valleys' in the countryside. The water has percolated down through cracks and pores, and even quite substantial rivers have become known for their disappearing acts. The Lathkill is kept above ground at its lower end by artificial 'puddling' with clay and, only in very wet weather, does the Manifold remain in its bed throughout its course. This greatly irritated one local nineteenth-century squire — clearly no geologist — who tried to plug the 'swallets' into which it sank near Wetton. The dry valleys were formed during the much colder conditions of the Ice Ages when water could flow and carve a course on the frozen subsoil.

As the water descends, it dissolves the limestone along its joints and cracks, enlarging them en route into passages and caves. Some 250 caves are known in the Peak, prompting Sir Arthur Conan Doyle to describe the scenery as 'hollow country'. He continued that: 'Could you strike it with some gigantic hammer, it would boom like a drum or possibly cave in altogether'. Most, though, are small and short and only a few are open to the public — four at Castleton, one at Bradwell, two at Matlock, and one at Buxton. Their distribution is not haphazard and occurs at the junction of the grit with the limestone. Some still contain active underground streams; others have been abandoned but rainfall still percolates through from the surface. This contains dissolved lime which precipitates out again as it emerges through the cave roof, gradually building an elongated cone of solid stone known as a stalactite. Some falls to the floor and the process is reversed to form stalagmites. The colour may vary from cream, orange, red, and even green or blue depending on any impurities in the rock.

There are also many surface caves beside the rivers in the Peak, some cut before the valleys were deepened by increased erosion after the Ice Ages and now left high above the valley floor. Prominent among these is Thor's Cave in the Manifold Valley. This and many others were used by early humans and have yielded valuable archaeological finds. Glacial meltwater greatly increased the formation of caves, sometimes enlarging a chamber until it could no longer support its own roof. This happened at Cave Dale, near Castleton which, until 200 years ago, had a natural roof over the entrance. Some geologists maintain that Winnats Pass was formed in the same way but this is open to dispute. At Cucklet Delf in Eyam are the relics of an ancient cave system, now reduced to a series of arches, and which was used for outdoor services during the plague of 1665-66.

largely responsible for the remaining ³/₄ of the area with the Kinder Scout Plateau forming the highest point at 2088 feet. It is difficult to imagine now the conditions prevailing at the time these rocks were formed. About 350 million years ago England was unrecognisable, part of a huge land mass experiencing tropical conditions just south of the equator. The area we now call the Peak was covered with a clear, shallow lagoon some 25 miles long and 10 miles wide occupied by forests of sea-lilies and other organisms, such as worms, molluscs, and myriads of microscopic sea creatures. As they died, they sank to the bottom where their bodies and shells accumulated into a layer of fine mud and sediment. This built up over a period of 35 million years or so and be-

Millstones at Bole Hill quarry, near Hathersage.

came compacted under its own weight. Because the sea floor was gently subsiding, the deposits did not choke the waters of the lagoon, and the limestone amassed to great thicknesses. At Eyam, it has been found to be 7000 feet thick.

A similar process occurred in the deeper open ocean, separated from the lagoon by its fringing ring of coral reef. The reef is particularly rich in fossils, and formed a harder rock more resistant to erosion. This has given prominent, upstanding areas of limestone — such as that above and around Castleton — and the only real hills and 'peaks' of the area, such as Thorpe Cloud, Bunster Hill, Chrome Hill, and Parkhouse Hill. At times, this tranquil scene was

11

shattered by the eruption of molten rock from submarine vents and volcanoes which spread their lava on top of the newly forming limestone. These thin layers of dark basalt are given the curious local name of 'toadstone', possibly because its dark-green, speckled coloration resembles the skin of a toad or possibly thus called by lead miners who dismissed the useless rock as 't'owd stone'! An outcrop can be seen in Cave Dale on **Walk 4**. Vents of ancient volcanoes form small, rounded hills at Castleton, Grange Mill west of Matlock, and at Hopton and Kniveton Wood near Wirksworth. The limestone was also injected with hot, mineral-bearing solutions that occupied cavities in the rock. As the material cooled, veins of lead, fluorspar, calcite, barytes, and copper formed in the parent rock. These have long attracted human attention, and attempts to extract these from the earth has had considerable impact on the scenery of the Peak.

The origin of the shale and grit lay some 200 miles to the north in part of a huge landmass that was later destined to emerge as Scotland. This was tilted and formed

The National Park adopted the millstone as its logo.

Fossils

Because the very rock itself is made up of the remains of long dead creatures, it is not difficult to find fossils on exposed limestone surfaces. Look for them among the individual stones of the dry stone walls or, better still, in the rock comprising the numerous 'squeezer' type stiles to be found in the White Peak.

The Carboniferous sea was home to many types of organism which used the dissolved calcium carbonate in the water to form their bones and shells. The most common species in the lagoon were brachiopods, corals, and crinoids. The most distinctive were the sea lilies, animals which grew on a stalk made up of rings of lime that could reach up to 8 or 10 feet in length. On top of this were five frond-like arms that wafted in the gentle currents to catch the small creatures on which it fed. They were related to the modern starfish and, when they died, their stalks left unusual ringed impressions that have earned them the name of 'Derbyshire screws'. They shared their environment with worms, sea weeds and shellfish. Among these were the lamp shells, especially attractive creatures that could grow up to a foot

or more in diameter.

The reefs were built up by myriads of polyps and are particularly rich in fossils. Brachiopods and calcareous algae — similar to modern seaweed — were very common, but hundreds of different species have been recorded including goniatites and trilobites. Many are strange to our eyes but a few bear some resemblance to modern creatures. Among these are the goniatites with their beautifully coiled shells — ancestors of the pearly nautilus found today in the Pacific. In contrast, the deeper, muddier waters outside the reef contained fewer marine animals and were inhabited largely by ostracods, goniatites, and bivalve molluscs.

'Derbyshire screws'.

southerly flowing rivers that brought fine mud, sand, and grit into the shallow sea then covering the Peak and the Pennines. These were later compressed into shale, the softest rock of the trio that has greatly influenced the course of the more major rivers, such as the Derwent in the east. Further earth movements raised the northern highlands, and the ensuing more vigorous erosion brought down coarser, heavier sediments of sands and gravels that later formed the gritstone. This forms the well-known upstanding 'Edges' that are a feature on both flanks of the Peak. Those in the west are more complex compared to their eastern counterparts where, from Derwent Edge in the north to Beeley Moor in the south, the grit stretches in a series of irregular 'steps' for 12 miles. It weathers along joints into weirdly shaped outcrops or tors that have correspondingly evocative names, such as the Boxing Glove Stones, Cakes of Bread, Wheelstones, and Salt Cellar. Its rough, abrasive texture made it ideal for grinding flour and it is commonly known as Millstone Grit. Later, it was used for sharpening the products made in the cutlery and steel mills of Sheffield. The introduction of artificially made abrasives led to the demise of the millstone makers and, beneath the eastern edges, hundreds of abandoned or incomplete stones are scattered below the walls of solid grit from whence they came.

The National Park adopted the millstone as its official logo in recognition of the historical importance of the industry. In reality, though, events were more complex as both the Peak and the more northerly land mass repeatedly rose and fell, resulting in alternating layers of shales and sandstones. This is seen to great effect on the eastern face of Mam Tor, exposed by a huge landslip caused by the unstable nature of the rocks. Other examples can be seen on **Walk 5** at Alport Castles and at Lud's Church on **Walk 11**. The appearance of the Peak changed according to the conditions prevailing at the time. When it was raised above sea-level, it would have formed a scenery of sandbanks, mud flats, or swamp. This was colonised by spores and seeds blown by the wind from the north, forming forests of giant ferns up to 60 feet high. The remains of these and other plant material formed a deep layer of peat that became compressed under ensuing deposits and chemically changed into coal. It outcrops only occasionally in the Peak — keep an eye open in the Goyt Valley on **Walk 8** around Derbyshire Bridge and on Goldsitch Moss on **Walk 11**. It never

Riches from the Earth

Millions of years ago, hot, mineral-rich solutions circulated through fissures and cracks within the limestone of the White Peak. The mixture cooled and crystallised into valuable minerals such as galena (lead ore), fluorspar, barytes, and calcite. For over 2000 years lead mining was an important part of the region's economy, but has declined this century with the advent of cheap imported sources of the metal. Ironically, commercial mining in the Peak became concentrated on the extraction of fluorspar, once the lead miner's waste or 'gangue' material. In fact, over the last seventy years mining companies have removed many of the major spoil heaps to reclaim the fluorspar. The White Peak is the source of three-quarters of Britain's fluorspar which is now used by the chemical industry for the production of fluorides, and by the steel industry as a flux. A new mine has just been approved at Great Hucklow. Barytes is used as a filler in paint and by the oil production industry as a drilling lubricant in oil wells. Calcite finds a use as gravel in paths.

The main mineral resource of the Peak is the limestone itself, quarried at numerous sites throughout the area, and a long-running source of controversy between conservationists and industry. There is no doubt that the quarries detract from the beauty of the Park, and the great lorries that serve them put a strain on the roads and villages through which they pass. There is also concern that the limestone — almost chemically pure calcium carbonate and useful to the chemical and cement industries — is a valuable resource squandered mainly on road construction. Reducing production would be highly controversial, however, because about 20 per cent of jobs in the Peak are dependent on quarrying, and it would be costlier to obtain road stone from alternative sources.

amassed into the thick seams found in the coalfields outside the National Park, and the mining occurred mainly on a local scale. Nevertheless, the period and rocks so far discussed are classed by geologists as belonging to the Carboniferous — or coal-forming — period.

Peakland Gems

A unique set of geological circumstances in the Castleton area makes it the only location of a beautiful banded fluorspar known as Blue John. Natural oils have made it predominantly blue, purple, and white, but there are many subtle variations of colour. It is not known for certain when it was first mined but the earliest record dates from the seventeenth century. It has been used since for ornaments and for jewellery. All the veins are found in Treak Cliff and, at their acme, produced 20 tons annually. The remaining deposits occur in thin veins, and production is down to half a ton or less — nowadays the mines make more money from visitors. The unusual name may come from the French bleu-jaune — 'blue

Blue John Cavern.

yellow' — or from lead miners wishing to differentiate it from 'black jack', their term for zinc blende.

Ashford Marble is another Peakland speciality. It is not a true marble but is formed from bituminous impurities in the limestone. These give the stone a satin-black hue when polished and was greatly valued by the Victorians for ornaments and inlay work. It is found in the vicinity of Ashford in the Water and may have been used very early indeed, for pieces of the dressed stone have been found in nearby burial mounds. It was certainly mined in the sixteenth century and, in 1748, a marble works was established near Ashford. These closed in 1905 and no quarries are currently in operation.

After the events of the Carboniferous, the Peak was transformed into a hot desert before becoming submerged under the sea once again for around 100 million years. Little is known for certain of events in the area after this time until the onset of the last major geological event to affect the Peak during the Ice Ages beginning about a million years ago. The tremendous erosive power of the ice and its melt water to grind, transport, and finally carve what lay in its path added the finishing touches to the ancient landscape and moulded its features into the form we recognise today. Up to this time, there were none of the dales and caves typical of the modern limestone scenery. The Peak, however, was not as heavily glaciated as the Lake District or the Yorkshire Dales, and was only covered in ice on two occasions. Furthermore, the glaciers had already spent much of their force further north and had greater depositional than erosive effect which is why there is an absence of U-shaped valleys and corries.

The ice transported its load of ground-up rocks and stones — called till — southwards on to the limestone plateau. This, together with fine wind-borne silt picked up by winds blowing from northern Europe, forms the basis of the soil of the White Peak. Unlike the Yorkshire Dales, the Peak escaped glaciation during the last ice advance and kept these fertile

deposits. The resulting pleasant green pasture contrasts starkly with the bare limestone scars and pavements of the Dales. During this time the Peak experienced a very severe tundra climate that froze the subsoil. Substantial amounts of summer meltwater was thus able to flow across the limestone and carve out valleys which today may have a very small stream or no water in them at all. These dry valleys are a characteristic feature of limestone scenery as, too, are the caves that developed during the warmer periods between the glaciers. They were used as dens by the predatory mammals of the day — bears, wolves, hyenas among them — that consumed their prey in the shelter of the cave. Bones of horses, deer, reindeer, mammoth, and woolly rhino have been discovered. Remnants of flints indicate that Paleolithic people also used the caves, those in the Manifold Valley and upper Dovedale being particularly favoured.

The human factor

When the Ice Age ended around 10,000 years ago, the Peak was a cold and relatively barren place. Pollen analysis has revealed an alpine flora but, apart from this, there were only a few stunted trees of arctic willow and hazel and low-lying sedges and mosses. The human population would only have numbered a few dozen. They hunted widely for their food and there is evidence that they cleared patches of ground by burning and felling to improve their chances of locating game. This represents the first significant human impact on the environment because, by decreasing the number of trees — and therefore also the take-up of water — the spread of peat bog over the moors may have been assisted. Gradually, though, the climate improved and other species began to colonise the area. Initially aspen, hairy birch, juniper, and then silver birch and rowan began to establish themselves. There was also a greater variety of flowers and, by the Boreal Period (7500-5500 BC) the Peak was lightly wooded with an open covering of Scots pine, birch and hazel.

Eventually the climate ameliorated sufficiently to encourage the spread of oak,

Lud's Church, where the alternating layers of shales and sandstones have been exposed by landslips.

Dry stone walls

Perhaps the most distinctive and the most widespread human contribution to the upland scene are the miles of stone walls that segment the countryside into geometrical parcels of land. Stone is not only the most appropriate material to use, it is also the only viable option. Hedgerows become difficult or impossible to establish on the higher ground, post and wire fencing is expensive to install and less durable — many dry stone walls have stood for centuries. Moreover, the stone is easily to hand and comes from the local vicinity. Thus, the walls reflect the local geology and those of dark-brown hue indicate their location in shale or grit country.

A lot of labour is involved in wall construction and they were not built just to look pretty. They became more extensive in the Middle Ages as a result of the growing importance of sheep rearing. The first walls simply divided one vast sheep run from another, helping to control the movement of the flocks. They also protected the arable land and provided shelter for the animals. Dry stone walling was used much earlier, though, and at Roystone Grange are rows of large 'orthostats' typical of the Roman period. Later medieval walls were built from rough-hewn boulders while modern walling from the eighteenth century to present times consists of stones carefully layered in size with the

This dry stone walling, near Litton, is a visible sign of the local geology.

smallest at the top and the whole capped with a row of coping stones.

Few of the early walls are still in existence and most were erected after the passing of the Enclosure Acts between 1760 and 1830. Typically, field walls are around 4 feet 6 inches high, about 27 inches wide at the bottom but tapering towards the top. They are built upon one or two foundation courses with a rubble filling and occasional 'through' stones to give strength. In places a gap would be left at the base as a 'creep hole' for the sheep. Interestingly, those in very old walls are too small for the larger modern breeds. To the observant, walls are also historical 'sermons in stone' in that the shape of the fields they enclose reveals their agricultural history. Long, narrow fields — sometimes with a reversed S shape — are 'fossilised' medieval strip fields. The relatively small, squarish fields of the limestone are younger and date mainly from the peak of the Enclosure awards during the eighteenth and nineteenth centuries. A third type occurs on the moorland — long straight walls forming large rectangular fields — and these resulted from the later systematic enclosure of the nineteenth century.

Walling is a traditional craft demanding considerable levels of skill and time. For this reason, walkers should always negotiate a wall via the stiles provided and never risk dislodging the stones by passing directly over the top.

The Bronze Age remains of Nine Ladies Stone Circle, Stanton Moor.

alder, elm, ash and lime into the sheltered valleys, and game animals began to occupy the more wooded areas. Such was the Peakland landscape that presented itself to the first agriculturalists around 3000 BC. These Neolithic people arrived from continental Europe bringing with them their domestic animals and seed corn, which they planted in the virgin soil of the cleared woodland. They favoured the light, well-drained grassy uplands of the limestone plateau, upon which they built the first settlements in the Peak. They also constructed chambered tombs to bury their dead, and these constitute the oldest monuments in the Peak. Five Wells, near Taddington, is the highest such tomb in Britain at over 1400 feet. This was one of the hundreds of barrows excavated by the famous nineteenth-century archaeologist, Thomas Bateman, who found evidence of at least twelve burials here. The most impressive Neolithic monument is Arbor Low, thought to have been a ceremonial religious site that probably entailed up to a million man hours and several years of building time. There must have been a high level of skill and organisation involved in the construction of these henges and, to this day, their exact purpose remains a mystery. There is evidence that Arbor Low and other sites, such as the Bull Ring at Dove Holes, may also have served as market and trading centres.

About 2000 BC, in the early Bronze Age, there was a further influx of immigrants from the Low Countries whose custom of including distinctively decorated pottery drinking vessels amongst grave goods has given them the name of Beaker Folk. Their introduction of bronze and improved metal working meant improved tools that cleared land for agriculture faster and more easily. They buried their dead in smaller round barrows, known as 'lows', an Anglo-Saxon word somewhat paradoxical in modern English because the burial mounds are usually sited on hill tops. The Beaker people extended their settlements on to the gritstone uplands, possibly as a result of population pressure or because of an improving climate, and began to clear the moorland from about 1750 BC. They seem to have particularly favoured the land east of the Derwent where, at Swine Sty above Curbar, can be found some of the best-preserved and most complete Bronze Age remains in the southern Pennines. Stanton Moor is particularly rich in these early remains, and more than seventy burial mounds are concentrated in this small area. They have been dated to around 1800-1400 BC and are associated with the nearby Nine Ladies Stone Circle, an important ritual site that can be seen on **Walk 10.**

Iron was introduced into Britain in the seventh century but it is not known when it made its first appearance in the Peak. More likely there was a gradual transition into the Iron Age which, although it lasted for about 700 years, has left remarkably few artefacts. The main archaeological legacy are the earthworks of the hillforts, which range in size from ½ acre to 16 acres. The largest and most impressive — although it is thought to pre-date the Iron Age — caps the summit of Mam Tor but, sadly, it has now partly disappeared down the unstable hillside. Other notable examples occur at Combs Moss, near Chapel en le Frith and Ball Cross, near Bakewell. Carl Wark above Hathersage was built upon an easily defended rocky knoll and is probably of Iron Age origin. The relatively sophisticated construction involved in the ramparts, however, seems to be of much later date. Interestingly, only one hillfort has been identified on the limestone at Fin Cop in Monsal Dale — an enigma as yet unexplained. The hillforts may be misnamed for there is evidence that they performed other than defensive functions. Some seem to have contained settlements and buildings, and it is quite feasible that they also served as administrative or agricultural trading centres.

Around the second century BC there was an influx of continental invaders, and the region became dominated by the chariot-driving Brigantes. In about 70 AD these people buckled under the Imperial might of the Roman legions, who established two forts in the Peak to control and subdue the natives. Very little remains of the fort of Navio, near present-day Brough, but it constitutes the most major settlement left behind by the Empire. Its 2-acre site probably housed a garrison of around 500 men, posted to defend the valuable Roman lead mining concerns in the Peak. The other fort, known as Ardotalia, lay just outside Glossop, and the Romans connected the two with a road which ran over the peat bogs of Bleaklow and Kinder Scout. It is partly exposed along the section known as Doctor's Gate, although the stone kerbs and slabs are of medieval date.

Buxton was important to the bath-loving Romans, and they built roads connecting it to Navio — crossing Bradwell Moor and still known as Batham Gate — and to the regional centre at Little Chester. They built other roads, including that partly followed by the A515, but the system is not extensive and there are curious gaps in the communication network they established. They were undoubtedly greatly attracted to the rich lead deposits, reputedly so plentiful in places that it could be extracted by shovel. The Peak was a very important source of the metal for the Romans as indicated by the discovery of numerous ingots or 'pigs' stamped with the Roman 'Lutudarum'. Although these were unearthed in the Matlock vicinity, the exact location of Lutudarum has never been proven conclusively. Many believe it to be the ancient settlement of Wirksworth, while the name may equally apply to a region of the Peak. It would seem that the British co-habited relatively peacefully with their Roman overlords, probably engaged in the traditional dual activities of mining and farming. There are relatively few remains of the period but traces of Romano-British fields, walls, and buildings may be observed on the archaeological trail at Roystone Grange, between Parwich and Pikehall.

There is a similar dearth of material from the Dark Ages that ensued after the withdrawal of the legions in the early fifth

Jane Eyre and Hathersage

Charlotte Brontë visited Hathersage in 1845 and it is thought that she subsequently used many of the buildings and local families as models for her setting and characters in Jane Eyre. *She stayed for three weeks with her friend at the vicarage and, during that time, explored the village and the surrounding moors. It is known that she visited Moorseats, just a short walk from the vicarage, and this could well be the Moor House in the novel to which Jane fled from Thornfield. Thornfield itself is thought to be North Lees Hall, one of the seven houses built by Robert Eyre for his sons around Hathersage. Charlotte could have been impressed by the long lineage of this local family, their history, and brasses in the church, and they would seem to be the source of the heroine's surname.*

The fictitious village name of Morton may have been inspired by the landlord of The George — a Mr Morton — who would have greeted the coach in which Charlotte arrived. Unlike her home town of Haworth, the mills of Morton made needles and one of the proprietors in the novel is called Mr Oliver, another well-known name in the real village.

There are other connections between Hathersage and the book, and it is possible to visit many of the places mentioned in the novel. It was published in 1847 just two years after Charlotte's visit so perhaps she may have begun the story while still in the village.

Leisure trails

There are five trails in the Peak District which follow the beds of old railways. These are owned by both local and/or the National Park authority and are available to walkers, cyclists, and horse riders provided certain byelaws are observed. The first to be converted was the Tissington Trail, a section of the former Buxton-Ashbourne line, opened in 1894 and finally closed in 1967. It was a branch line and, at one time, carried milk from Hartington to London, as well as transporting limestone to Buxton and providing a local passenger service. The Park authority purchased an 11-mile section of the line in 1968, covered the rough ballast with quarry overburden and seeded it with grass to make a trail suitable for walkers and cyclists. Reclamation by nature has been so successful that parts of the trail are now nature reserves!

The High Peak Trail, formerly the Cromford and High Peak Line, was purchased in 1971 and joins the Tissington Trail at Parsley Hay. The Monsal and Manifold trails are undoubtedly the most spectacular as they run through deep limestone gorges. The Monsal Trail — the former Midland Railway — closely follows the valley of the Wye and was opened in 1980. Four of its tunnels are closed, making the route incomplete, and some of the linking routes are difficult, but the paths are rewarding.

Further north, the Sett Valley Trail, purchased by Derbyshire County Council from British Rail in 1973, provides a pleasant, 2-mile, traffic-free link between New Mills and Hayfield. As with most of the trails, cycle hire centres provide the motorist with the perfect opportunity to leave the car behind and explore, and leaflets giving suggested walking and cycling routes are available from dispensers or local information centres.

The High Peak Trail joins the Tissington Trail at Parsley Hay, providing excellent cycling for all ages.

century. There are few documents, and the earliest English record of the Peak is a seventh-century tax assessment called The Tribal Hidage. This is the first reference to the people of the area as the Pecsaetan — dwellers of the Peak — after whom the region is named. It was a Pecsaetan warrior that Bateman discovered at Benty Grange, buried in the late seventh century with a precious collection of grave goods that included an iron helmet. The helmet is unusual in that it incorporated pagan and Christian symbols and must have been made during the transition period from 'Dark Ages' to Christianity.

Christianity arrived in the middle of the seventh century, and the Saxon crosses of Eyam, Bradbourne, Bakewell, and Hope are among the most important remains of the period in the Peak. They are believed to have been preaching crosses, of which more than thirty survive, marking sites of worship before the churches were built. Of these, little now remains, and even the Domesday Book only mentioned three churches in 1086. In fact, the Saxons made a possibly greater contribution to the Peakland landscape through their language. Their influence can be seen in many place names, and constitutes virtu-

Dams and reservoirs

Some consider the solid dams and the artificial lakes with their conifer-clad banks to be an unwelcome intrusion on the Peakland scene. To birdwatchers, sailors, and fishermen, however, they present opportunities to pursue their hobby. Of the fifty or so reservoirs in the Peak, none is better known than those of the Derwent valley. There are now three but originally six were planned to supply Derby, Nottingham, Leicester, and Sheffield with drinking water. Howden was started in 1901 and completed in 1912 to be followed by Derwent Dam in 1916. The large workforce of 'navvies' was housed during these fifteen years in a self-contained community at Birchinlee between the two dams. It was built largely of corrugated iron and came to be known as 'Tin Town'; although it housed up to 1000 people, there is little trace of it now. Demand was still not satisfied, however, and in 1935 work began on a third dam downstream. Ladybower Reservoir was completed in 1945 with a capacity of 6,300,000,000 gallons but necessitated the destruction of villages at Ashopton and Derwent. The villagers were rehoused in specially built accommodation at Yorkshire Bridge, just below the earthwork dam.

A few of the dams have failed and have had to be rebuilt. Carsington is the most recent example but the first incident was the collapse of the dam impounding Bilberry Reservoir in 1852, during which eighty-one people were killed. Britain's worst flooding disaster occurred twelve years later with the failure of the newly built Dale Dyke Dam. Around 700 million cubic feet of water surged down the valley with the loss of 240 lives.

Today, the reservoirs attract many visitors in their own right, so many in fact that the Park has had to introduce traffic management schemes, car parks, and picnic areas. Purpose-made trails and paths have also been provided, and considerable resources have been invested to landscape the banks of the reservoirs and in the provision of public facilities. The restriction of vehicles at peak times of the year around the Goyt Valley and Derwent Reservoirs makes it possible to enjoy a gentle stroll beside the water at even the busiest times.

Fernilee Reservoir, not far from Buxton.

ally the only method of tracing their progress across the Peak. Revealed, for instance, is the extent of forest clearance and the fact that most settlements were established before Domesday in 1086. The Peak at this time was a frontier zone between the kingdoms of Mercia and Northumbria. The Vikings invaded Britain from about 830 AD but place-name evidence suggests they made little progress west of the Derwent. Then, in 920 AD, a significant historical event occurred at Bakewell when Edward the Elder, son of Alfred the Great, brought together the leaders of all the kingdoms and factions in the country and was subsequently chosen as overlord. He could thus be called the first monarch of the British Isles.

Likewise, the Normans have left few visible reminders of their rule. Some churches contain elements of Norman work and similarly little remains of their secular building. There are remains of a motte-and-bailey castle at Pilsbury, near Hartington but the most extensive monument of the Conquest is Peveril Castle and the planned town of Castleton which it overlooks. The castle served as an administrative centre and hunting lodge for the most dominant feature of the Norman landscape. This was the Royal Forest of the Peak, an area of some 180 square miles set aside exclusively for the pleasure of the King's hunt. This was the largest of several Forests established wholly or partly in the Peak. Macclesfield Forest impinged on the lower Dane Valley and Duffield Frith occupied land in the southeast. There is little trace of the Royal Forest today but it remained a major feature of the landscape for 500 years

The twelfth and thirteenth centuries were a time of agricultural expansion with the creation of many new villages and farms. Hartington received the first market charter in the Peak in 1203 and others followed at Tideswell in 1251 and Monyash in 1340. From the twelfth to the fourteenth centuries there was a great increase in sheep and wool production. The monasteries in particular took a great interest in the new farming, and were already exporting wool by the thirteenth century. Often, the monasteries themselves were situated far outside the Peak, and the stockrearing was undertaken by lay brothers in outlying farms known as granges. The monks owned almost fifty granges in the Peak, and the wealth generated from wool, together with the proceeds from lead mining, funded the building of outstanding parish churches such as at Bakewell and Tideswell

A familiar Peak District sight — sheep grazing near Kinder Scout.

The conversion to sheep necessitated enclosing the land and the construction of walls to control the flocks. These early walls may have followed the old boundaries of the medieval strips, as at Chelmorton and Litton. In these cases the fields are long and narrow, sometimes preserving the reversed S shape where the plough team turned at the end of their run. The enclosures also served to depopulate the countryside and this, together with the devastations of the Black Death in the fourteenth century, led to many deserted villages. Arable farming still continued, though — often in the large open field system — and the traditional ridge and furrow can still be seen around the Peak at Tissington and Bradbourne, among other places. Even before the heyday of the Enclosure Movement in the eighteenth and nineteenth centuries, Celia Fiennes was wont to remark of the Peak that '...you see neither hedge nor tree but only low drye stone walls round some ground...'. Gradually, hundreds of miles of walls were built on the pasture, heath, and common land dividing the land into the familiar chequer-board patterns we see today. The prosperity of the Middle Ages affected many landowning families who built substantial residences with their new affluence. Many of the fine manor houses seen today, such as the Halls at Eyam, Tissington, Hartington, and North Lees near Hathersage, have their origins in this period.

The other great mainstay of the Peakland economy was lead, known to have been mined since Roman times. Ingots inscribed with 'Lutudarum' have been found as far away as Sussex and, although mining may have declined after the Romans left, Saxon smelting sites were noted in Domesday Book at Bakewell, Wirksworth,

Lead mining

Lead ore or galena is found throughout the White Peak. It was injected as a hot, mineral-rich solution into cracks and cavities in the limestone millions of years ago and, as it cooled, it crystallised out along fissures in the rock. The larger veins are known as 'rakes' and can run for several miles at widths of up to 10 feet. Smaller offshoots are called 'scrins'. The workings along the rakes — which can be up to 500 feet deep — were frequently screened off by a line of trees planted to keep away inquisitive animal and human visitors.

Anyone could become a miner but there were certain laws and customs that had to be obeyed. These evolved over the centuries but the framework was laid down as early as 1288. The laws were administered by the Barmaster and a jury of twelve miners from the Barmote Courts which met regularly to adjudicate local disputes and to record the mining activities of an area. Miners were subject to a rigid and sometimes harsh set of rules. For instance, lead could not be taken from churchyards, orchards, gardens, or highways. Any new vein had to be paid for by a 'freeing dish' of ore to the Barmaster before it could be worked and a miner had to work his claim regularly or risk having it 'nicked' or taken from him. Stealing another man's ore was a grave offence and anyone caught three times could be starved to death or lose a hand.

Using only simple hand tools, and candles for lighting, it was dangerous and uncomfortable work. By the seventeenth century, many mines had reached the water table and required the construction of drainage channels, or 'soughs'. These were bored by hand through the hills and out into a suitable river valley and, as can be imagined, they were very expensive and time consuming to complete. They did not all prove cost effective and many companies were ruined in the process. One of the first was the Cromford Sough cut in 1690 at a cost of £33,000 to drain Gang Mine. It was later ingeniously used by Arkwright to power his second cotton mill in Cromford. During the early nineteenth century, steam-powered pumps were installed and used with some success but could not halt the decline of the industry in the later nineteenth and twentieth centuries.

Whose park is it anyway?

The Peak District was designated a National Park in 1951, the first of eleven such parks now in existence in England and Wales. It is managed by the independent and autonomous Peak Park Joint Planning Board consisting of over thirty members. Of these, two-thirds are appointed by local county and district councils with the remainder representing interested parties and appointed by the Minister of State for the Environment. The Board operates on a tight budget of about 2.6 million pounds a year, and has to perform something of a juggling act to try to fulfil its varied financial and management responsibilities. It faces several difficulties in its role as guardian of the nation's heritage. These arise because the Peak is far more than an outdoor leisure park — it is a landscape in which 40,000 people live and work. Indeed, much of the charm of the Peak comes from the thriving communities and the fact that the villages have not descended into manicured weekend retreats.

It may come as a surprise to learn that the Park itself only owns about 4 per cent of the land. The National Trust owns 10 per cent and the Water Boards have 15 per cent. The remainder is in private hands but the Board has successfully negotiated access agreements and concessionary footpaths for the public. The Park has set up a Ranger Service with twenty-four full-time staff. These are assisted by 170 part-timers and 200 volunteers who make a valuable contribution in the day-to-day running of the Park. Losehill Hall was the first residential National Park study centre in the country when it opened in 1972. It provides information on the Park and training in rural skills. The authorities have also established eight Information Centres which distribute leaflets on all aspects of the Peak and also the free newspaper Peakland Post.

Bakewell puddings

It would be difficult to find a town more appropriately named than Bakewell, for it is the birth place of the famous culinary accident that led to a hitherto untried combination of strawberry jam, eggs, butter, and flaky pastry that we know today as Bakewell Pudding. Ironically, the recipe resulted from a near disaster in the kitchen of the Rutland Arms in the 1850s when some visiting gentry ordered a jam tart. Evidently the cook was very busy and, in the heat of the moment, mistakenly spread the jam first and poured the egg mixture on top. The resulting sweet-tasting pudding was greatly appreciated by the distinguished guests and thereafter appeared regularly on the menu.

Unfortunately, the name of the original cook is unknown but she did bequeath the recipe in her will. Again, the name of the beneficiary is a mystery and has caused some rivalry between two local bakeries who each claim the 'secret' formula for the pudding. One of these is the Old Original Pudding Shop in Bridge Street, with its equally quaint and attractive sign, built in the seventeenth century as a chandler's shop. The wife of the chandler, Mrs Wilson, is said to have grasped the commercial potential — and the recipe itself — very early. The other bakery in Matlock Street claims to have received the recipe from the man who helped the cook write her will. Whoever is right, the produce from both establishments is equally delicious but always ask for puddings, never tarts — the locals are quite fussy over the name of their speciality — and expect something quite different from the easily obtained commercial products bought off supermarket shelves.

Ashford, and Matlock. It would have been in considerable demand for roofing during the great medieval building period, but mining operations remained on a relatively small scale. Extraction of 't'owd man' — as the lead was called by the Peakland miners — was strictly regulated by the Barmote Courts who met regularly to administer justice and settle disputes under their own codes of practise. In fact, the miners were almost a law unto themselves and could, for instance, mine without the landowner's consent. In the event of a find they had automatic access to the nearest running water and highway.

Lead was relatively easy to mine in the Peak and commanded good prices. In the years of greatest activity from around 1700-1750, there were at least 10,000 miners working the veins, and it seems that every field in the White Peak contains the irregular hummocks and hollows of old workings. There may be as many as 50,000 abandoned shafts, often concealed by undergrowth, and walkers are consequently advised not to stray from the

Cycling in the Peak District

With such interesting and varied scenery and a good density of minor roads and bridlepaths, the Peak District cannot fail to attract the cyclist's interest. With half the population of England living within a two-hour drive of the National Park, however, and plenty of general through traffic between the industrial centres to east and west, main roads connecting important tourist centres can be very busy. The cyclist, therefore, has to contend with large numbers of cars over weekends and bank holidays and heavy lorries — many of them from the numerous quarries in the White Peak — during the weekdays. Fortunately, most of the traffic tends to be confined to the major routes and, although the tours were compiled with mainly the motorist in mind, Tours 1, 2, 3, 4, and 7 are suitable for cyclists.

Take into account not only the distance but the undulating nature of the terrain, and allow a good day for each ride. The cyclist need not be confined to the roads either. With the 'invention' of mountain bikes has come an interest in off-road routes using green lanes, bridlepaths (but not footpaths), and trails such as the Tissington, High Peak, Monsal,

footpaths. Flooding became a major problem as the workings progressed further underground and many mines became uneconomic. The industry went into a decline and, by the 1950s, had virtually ceased under the added competition from cheaper foreign sources and the recycling of existing reserves.

Lead was not the only mineral mined in the Peak. The copper mines at Ecton were especially productive, and at the peak of production in 1786, 4000 tons of ore were

A beautiful relic of the Industrial Revolution — the steam engine at Middleton Top.

Manifold, and Sett Valley. Many of these are also suitable for sturdy road bikes. Study the relevant maps and, often, interesting circular routes can be devised. Remember, however, that these trails and bridlepaths are shared with walkers, so be prepared to slow down and pass carefully, especially when approaching from behind, as you may not have been heard.

There are now many cycle hire centres in the Peak District where the motorist may leave the car and take to the saddle (see useful address section) for a modest hire fee.

extracted by 300 miners. Limestone was quarried in increasing amounts, at first on a small scale but gradually organised on a larger scale with the growing agricultural demand and improved transport. Production has continued, and it makes a significant contribution to the Peakland economy today. Gritstone, too, was extracted from the hillside, initially for local mills but later for use as grindstone in the cutlery and steel trades in Sheffield.

The Industrial Revolution could be said to have started in the Peak with the arrival of Richard Arkwright at Cromford in 1771. Here, in this somewhat unlikely setting, he built the world's first water-powered cotton mill and embarked on an industrial enterprise so successful that, within twenty years, he could claim a personal fortune sufficient to wipe out the national debt! It is interesting to consider that had Arkwright's achievements been followed up, then Cromford and not Manchester may have become the centre of the nation's cotton industry. What attracted men like Arkwright and Jedediah Strutt was the available water power of the Derwent, describe as a 'fury of a river' by Daniel Defoe. It had been used for centuries, of course, to grind corn and lead but was not put to large-scale industrial use until Arkwright introduced his new methods in the eighteenth century.

Arkwright built three mills in Cromford,

Well dressing

Well dressing is virtually confined to the Peak — a thanksgiving ceremony for the precious gift of water on the dry limestone. Little else is known, for the origin and history of this mysterious custom are veiled in the mists of time. It may have originated from pre-Roman pagan animal sacrifices to the water gods in gratitude for past supplies and as an inducement for future favours. The remoteness of the Peakland hills may have been a factor in its survival from successive waves of invading Romans, Saxons, Danes, and Normans. The early Christian church absorbed and adapted the tradition which consequently developed strong religious associations. Most of the pictorial themes are biblical, and a service to bless the wells is held in each village every year without fail.

There are no early records of the custom but it is known to have been revived at Tissington in the seventeenth century where the wells continued to provide water through a period of severe drought in 1615. The village is traditionally the first in the season to dress its wells on Ascension Day.

The method of dressing varies but always begins with the soaking of the wooden frames that will support the design. Holes and nails in the wood help key in the puddled clay which is spread evenly on top of the frame. The design, previously drawn on paper, is placed on the clay and pricked through with a sharp implement. The resulting outline is then filled with alder cones — 'black knobs' — berries, seeds or rice, and then filled in with bark, mosses, and lichens to give effective foreground, background, and shadow. The final process involves the delicate application of petals, starting from the bottom so that rain easily runs off the overlapping layers.

The amount of material and time involved is considerable and can take many villagers up to a week to dress one well. Some villages dress more than one well or even decorate street taps and standpipes. Some are very strict in the use of only natural materials but the results are always of a very high standard. Only fourteen villages observed the custom up to fifty years ago, but the number has since doubled. It has spread to other parts of the country in recent years but only two villages can claim any length of tradition outside the Peak.

Lumford Mill in Bakewell and the original Cressbrook Mill in the Wye Valley. There are other fine mills in the Peak, some built by owners of a less benevolent nature than Arkwright. He seems to have provided well for his employees, who were mostly women and children, and he constructed houses and public facilities for their well being. Conditions at some mills, such as Litton, were undoubtedly harsh, although the Memoirs of Robert Blincoe recounting the cruelty of his working days at the mill in the early nineteenth century, are now believed to have been deliberately distorted.

Transport routes in the Peak did not improve until the arrival of turnpikes in the middle of the eighteenth century. Until then, the Peak remained a remote upland with only basic communication with the rest of the country. Many traders and locals used ancient trackways, such as the Portway, or old packhorse routes. These became established in medieval times when long trains of horses carried loads of salt and cheese from Cheshire and returned with cargo as varied as lead, copper, lime, and cotton. Sometimes, as many as forty or fifty animals were involved and were led by 'jaggers' — so called after the German jaeger ponies they used. They are remembered at places like Jagger's Clough on Kinder Scout.

Special types of bridge were built to accommodate a single file of horses and the panniers carried on either side of the animal. These narrow bridges with their low parapets seem very quaint to modern eyes and form a very attractive element of the Peak landscape. Viator's Bridge at Milldale is a famous example and can be seen on **Walk 2**. Those at Ashford in the Water, Three Shires Head, Bakewell, and Edale are similarly worthy of note but they are not an uncommon sight in the Peak. Gradually, the situation improved with the introduction of turnpikes and, for the first time, there was a reasonable system of roads along which farm produce and minerals could be transported more rapidly and at less cost. Some of the new roads adopted sections of the old packhorse routes like the Snake Pass, built by Telford in 1821.

With no canals across the hilly terrain of the Peak, these roads carried all the traffic

until the coming of the railways in the nineteenth century. In fact, they arrived surprisingly early given the nature of the country over which they had to pass. The first to be laid was the Cromford and High Peak Railway in 1831, linking the Cromford Canal with the Peak Forest canal at Whaley Bridge. The most difficult projects were those routes that crossed the Peak east-west for they had to negotiate the high land in the centre of the region. Until 1860, the Midland line from London stopped at Rowsley, awaiting permission to push westwards through to Buxton. The delay was caused by the Dukes of Devonshire and Rutland, neither of whom wanted the railway through their estates. The line went ahead though after suggestions that it be laid underground through the Haddon estate and that special stations be constructed at Bakewell and Hassop for the Dukes. The 10-mile section through the Wye Valley that followed is perhaps the most famous stretch of old railway in the Peak, for it involved the construction of the impressive Monsal viaduct. The Pennines were traversed by two routes, one through Longdendale and

One of the many versions of the National Park logo.

the notorious Woodhead Tunnel in 1847, and the other through Edale and the Hope Valley. This line entailed the construction of the Cowburn and Totley tunnels and is now the only passenger route still working across the Peak. It opened in 1894 and, in the same year, a line was completed between Ashbourne and Buxton. Apart from the Hope Valley line, these railways were closed during the 1960s and have since been purchased by the Park and converted into walking and riding trails.

The last major impact on the Peakland landscape were the dams and reservoirs constructed to satisfy the industrial and domestic demands for water in the surrounding towns and cities. The high rainfall of up to 60 inches a year, and the deep valleys of the gritstone first caught the eye of the Victorian engineers in 1830 when the Sheffield Water Board constructed the first reservoir in the Peak on Hallam Moors. Sheffield was supplied by eight more reservoirs by 1881 by which time Manchester and the other large towns had also realised the Peak's potential. Today, there are over fifty reservoirs in the Park, the best known undoubtedly the triple dams of the upper Derwent, famous for their association with Barnes Wallace and the bouncing bomb during the World War II.

The National Park

There has been a price to pay, of course, in both financial and environmental terms. Several villages were flooded and, in the Derwent valley, Ashopton and Derwent village had to be sacrificed. Among the buildings was the seventeenth-century Derwent Hall while, in the Goyt Valley, the Victorian Errwood Hall disappeared under the waters of Errwood Reservoir. The

Fine walking country — the Pennine Way at Kinder Scout.

27

Eldon Quarry.

presence and construction of the reservoirs are controversial today because of modern attitudes to the environment. The twentieth century has witnessed a growing awareness of areas of outstanding natural beauty with the formation of organisations such as the National Trust in 1895. The Trust came to the Peak as early as 1906 when it purchased the Market Hall at Winster but, it was 1930 before it acquired its first land holding at Alport Height, near Wirksworth. Over the years it has been endowed with gifts and bequests that included Kinder Scout, the Hope Woodlands, parts of Dovedale, Mam Tor, and Winnats Pass until today it owns about 10 per cent of the land in the Park.

Now the Peak is regarded as part of our national heritage, there for all to enjoy. It is easy to forget that this has not always been the case and that, until fairly recent times, this beautiful landscape was denied to all but the privileged few. Pressure for access to the hills of the Peak was especially great because of the sheer numbers of people living in cities like Sheffield and Manchester around the fringes of the moors. It is no accident that the Peak was eventually the first area to be formally set aside as a National Park. During the harsh years of the 1920s and 1930s, many town dwellers sought escape from the daily grime and drudgery by

donning their sweaters and nailed boots and heading off for the clean air of the moors. The problem was that much of this was forbidden territory, managed as the exclusive preserve of the grouse and strictly guarded by stick-wielding gamekeepers who did not hesitate to evict forcibly unwelcome trespassers.

It has been calculated that, of approximately 150,000 acres of moorland in 1932, 110,000 acres were in private hands, 28,000 acres were owned by water boards and local authorities, and that only 1200 acres had adequate public access. An attempt had been made in 1884 to introduce an 'Access to the Mountains' Bill to give unrestricted rights to walk on uncultivated moor but it was stopped by the powerful land-owning lobby. Little progress was made after that and, with increasing unemployment and deteriorating conditions in the cities, frustrations mounted and the time was ripe for action. Matters came to a head in the Peak with the organised mass trespass in 1932 on to Kinder Scout, a well-publicised event that brought wider national awareness to the injustice of the situation. It proved to be a catalyst — a mass rally in Winnats Pass a few months later drew 10,000 supporters, and others followed in Surrey, Scotland, and Wales. Things could never be quite the same again.

The increasing national demand for public access eventually led to the National Parks and Access to the Countryside Act of 1949 and, two years later in April 1951, the Peak District was officially designated as Britain's first National Park. One of the first tasks of the new authority was to negotiate access to the former 'battlegrounds' of Kinder Scout and Bleaklow, and within a few years had established agreements for over 76 square miles of these northern moors. The public is now free to roam here except during the autumn grouse-shooting season. The boundary was drawn up to enclose 542 square miles of outstanding limestone and grit scenery, and its rather odd shape is a result of the exclusion of major limestone workings or areas of heavier industry. The Park is administered by the Peak Park Joint Planning Board that has a difficult task balancing all the demands made on the Peak by its visitors and inhabitants. On the one hand it has to provide for and cope with the sheer numbers of tourists who come to the Park. There are some 20 million leisure visits each year, perhaps not surprising when it is estimated that half the population of England lives within 60 miles of the Park boundary.

Part of the problem stems from the tendency of visitors to congregate around certain 'honey pots', and this has led to considerable traffic and erosion problems. Dovedale and Kinder Scout, in particular, have been seriously affected, and the Park has had to devise ways to alleviate the problems. On the other hand, it has to look after the needs of its 40,000 inhabitants and go some way towards satisfying the demand for its mineral resources. In fact, limestone extraction poses one of the major scenic threats to the Peak today and creates something of a dilemma for the Park authorities. Places like Eldon Hill quarry and the Hope Cement works are undoubted eyesores, but they were established long before the Park came into existence and also provide a considerable proportion of the 8000 or so jobs available in the Peak. The Park authorities have reacted to these seemingly conflicting interests in innovative and imaginative ways. The encouragement of integrated rural development programmes, the conversion of old railway routes to nature trails, the creation of traffic management schemes and close co-operation with the Forestry Commission, farmers, and Water Boards have proved very successful.

Formal recognition first came in 1966 with the award of the coveted Diploma for Nature Conservation by the Council of Europe. It has since won the award four times and would seem to justify the belief that the Park is well managed and that the future of this unique and precious part of our natural heritage is in safe hands.

The canal terminus at Cromford.

Natural history

The Peak District's unique position on the boundary between upland and lowland Britain is immediately noticeable in the appearance of wilder and more elemental scenery. There are many other features distinguishing the two landscapes but, from the natural history standpoint, the Peak's location at this physical crossroads has encouraged an unusual juxtaposition of species, several of which lie at the very limit of their geographical range. Within this larger setting are the contrasts inside the Peak itself for it is an area of varied geology and habitats. The central limestone core and the surrounding gritstone and shales have distinctive flora and fauna peculiar to that rock and soil. Moreover, conditions vary considerably between the high flat plateaus, the sloping hill sides, the valley floors, and the deep dales. All this amounts to a very interesting collection of species, some of which are rarities outside the Park.

Farmland

An important fact to remember when considering the Peakland landscape is that it is far from natural. From the earliest Neolithic farmers onwards, humans have managed and altered the environment for the improvement of food production and provision of resources. The peat bogs, the heather moors, the pasture, and the dry stone walls are the end result of thousands of years of land management. It is probable that the only truly natural landscape exists in areas inaccessible to grazing animals such as the limestone crags and rocky gritstone cloughs.

Farming, of course, has contributed greatly to the creation of the countryside we see today. On the sweet pastures of the limestone plateau, dairying and sheep farming have traditionally been the most important forms of agriculture, and it was to help control the stock that the miles of dry stone walls were erected. On the lower slopes, however, an increasing amount of land is being devoted to arable. Sheep are predominant on the grit moorland but they share the heather with red grouse. This bird has been popular sport for centuries, and it often generates more income from shooting rights than sheep rearing does. For this reason, it has had an enormous influence on the landscape of large stretches of upland Britain. Heather is vital to its lifecycle — it feeds on young shoots and nests among the older, woodier stems. The heather is periodically fired in the spring to encourage new growth and this creates a patchwork of colour on the hillside. It is easy to disturb the birds. They rise up suddenly and fly away with their distinctive flurry and glide, and their call of 'Go back, go back'. Every year, the twelfth of August heralds the start of the open season during which time certain of the access moors are closed in rotation. The Peak is home of two hardy kinds of mountain sheep bred to withstand the

Two areas of farmland: the Derwent Valley (opposite) and below the Chrome and Packhouse Hills (below).

The purple of the heather seen on Froggatt Edge.

winters of the high moors. The attractively named Dale o' Goyt, or Derbyshire Gritstone, is a speckle-faced animal originating in the west of the Peak. The Roman-nosed Whitefaced Woodland comes from the Woodlands Valley above Ladybower reservoir.

Heather and peat moors

Although they are imposed upon the land, farming methods have to be adapted to the natural environment and fall within the conditions set by the climate, soil, and rock. These same factors, of course, also affect the species and distribution of the plants and animals naturally occurring in the landscape. The grit underlies the heather and peat moors surrounding the comparatively lush green pastures of the limestone. It seems impossible that the rock beneath the wet, featureless peat bogs is both porous and rich in potash, but the high rainfall leaches any soluble material out of the soil. The flat plateaus are badly drained and are characterised by a seemingly endless expanse of dark acid peat. This has been eroded into upstanding 'hags' and intervening 'groughs', which to the walker and writer, John Hillaby, resembled the droppings of dinosaurs!

Peat bogs may seem quite natural today but the landscape would have looked quite different just a few thousand years ago. Peat, in fact, is the end result of a gradual degradation of the plant life from the deciduous forest that once covered the moors after the Ice Age. Remains of ancient trees are occasionally exposed in the

The emperor moth, part of the rich insect life of the grit moors.

The walker may be lucky to see one of the rare birds of prey, the peregrine falcon (left) and the hen harrier (right).

The Royal Forest of the Peak

This was the largest of the Royal Forests established by the Norman kings in the Peak. It is thought that the Saxons also used this north-western area for hunting but it was the Normans who first introduced official laws and administration. The boundaries of the Forest followed the Rivers Goyt and Etherow on the west and north, across the head of the Derwent which it then followed south-west to the foot of Bradwell Dale, to the Wye south of Tideswell and back to the Goyt. This substantial piece of territory covered about 180 square miles and was divided into three wards. One of these — Campagna — is significantly named for it originates from a French word meaning 'lightly wooded open country'.

'Forest' in medieval times referred to an area set aside for hunting, and not to the extent of tree cover. There was a variety of game available including wolves, wild boar, wild cat, the native red deer, and the fallow deer — which the Normans introduced themselves. Some of these animals are now extinct in the British Isles but are present in a few place names like Wildboarclough and Wolfscote Dale. The Forest was popular with a number of monarchs who made regular visits. Among these was Henry II, who repossessed and strengthened Peveril's Castle at Castleton. It was from here that the High Steward administered the Forest and enforced the harsh laws of vert and venison (the vegetation and deer). There were dire consequences for anyone caught with a killed animal, but no cases of capital punishment were recorded. Gradually, however, an expanding population required more land and fuel, and patches of cleared land, or 'assarts', nibbled away at the edges of the Forest. Lead smelting made increasing demands on the timber resource and, by the end of the fifteenth century, little remained of the original Forest. The Civil War wreaked the final ravage on timber and deer and the land was officially disafforested in 1674.

The Forest has left few traces but is remembered in several place names like Peak Forest and Chapel-en-le-Frith (frith was Old English for 'wood'). The Forest boundary was marked by stone crosses and those surviving at Hope, Wheston, and Edale may have been erected for this purpose.

Birds of the woodland areas of the Peak District include the pied flycatcher (top left) and nightjar (top right), whilst sparrowhawks (bottom left) and goshawks (bottom right) are attracted by the dark conifer plantations.

You may be lucky to see a lapwing soaring above the limestone pastures.

The slowworm can sometimes be found on the warm southern slopes.

tractively named cloudberry, a northern species here on its southern limit. It is rarely found below 2000 feet and can still be found on Kinder Scout and Bleaklow. It was once much more common, and its red fruit — similar to a raspberry — was harvested during the last century and sold in local markets.

The drier slopes below the summits support a more varied flora which is dominated by heather. It forms a vibrant purple blaze in mid-August and often grows in patches of different age. These result from the burning every eleven years or so which is undertaken for the benefit of the grouse. The heather also provides food for the mountain hare, a rabbit-sized creature that turns completely white in winter. It disappeared from the Peak after the Ice Age but was re-introduced during the last century for sporting purposes. There is also plenty of rough grassland on the slopes, characterised by the tough tussocks of mat grass — untouched even by sheep — and unfortunately increasing amounts of bracken.

Bilberry, crowberry, and cowberry prefer the drier ground further down, and their red and black fruits form an important food source for birds in the autumn. Bilberry is deciduous and its leaves take on a lovely orange tinge. Sheep are quite partial to a nibble, and it is not often allowed to develop its more usual bushy growth. Both crowberry and cowberry are evergreen plants and lie on their southern limit in the Peak.

At first glance the grit moors may seem devoid of animal life but nature rewards the patient. Among the rich insect life are the large emperor moth, with its distinctive eye markings on the wings, and the northern oak eggar whose dark brown and black caterpillars can be found in the heather. Of the few butterflies on the moors, the green hairstreak can be seen on the bilberry flowers in the spring together with the orange-tailed bumble bee. The most common birds are the meadow pipits and the red grouse, but curlew, dunlin, and twite are not rare. A species that is more often heard than seen is the ring ouzel which makes a 'chinking' sound resembling two pebbles being knocked together. The walker may be lucky to spot an occasional golden plover — handsome birds with gold, black, and white feathers. He or she may be even luckier and see one of the rare birds of prey. Merlin, peregrine falcons, goshawks, and hen harriers have been seen above the moors. Unfortunately, no golden eagles have returned to the Peak although they were recorded here in the seventeenth century.

sides of the groughs but the woods no longer grow on the surface because of a deterioration in the climate and the extensive clearances carried out by people. But the peat is not permanent either, and it is being badly eroded by water and wind. It is thought that some damage may have been caused by fires in recent dry periods and by overgrazing. Another cause is atmospheric pollution and the the 'acid rain' that originates from the industrial cities around the Peak. This has also greatly affected sensitive species such as sphagnum moss and lichens.

Hillaby regarded the peat to be botanically at 'the end of its tether', but the wetter bogs, springs, and seepage zones are characterised by a range of plants. These are dominated by hare's-tail cotton grass with its flowers resembling balls of cotton wool. This appearance may be the origin of the numerous 'featherbed mosses' of the high moors. Sphagnum moss may also be present, easily detected by its bright green colour, although this is becoming scarcer because of atmospheric pollution. Further colour may be added by the yellow star-shaped flowers of the bog asphodel. The sundew also makes an occasional appearance and it survives by supplementing its diet with insects attracted to its sticky red leaves. A particular speciality of the wetter moors is the at-

Place names in the Peak

The earliest place names come from the language of the British people who occupied the Peak long before the arrival of the Saxons and the Danes in the Dark Ages. Of the few that survive, river names are the most common — simple, evocative words such as *derva*, meaning oak, and the origin of the modern Derwent. Surprisingly, the Dove was thought to have been a dark river, and its name is derived from their word for black — *dubo*. 'Tor', which means a rocky hill, is also believed to be British, and it is a puzzle why the word only appears in the southern Pennines and the south-west. These people buried their dead in barrows later called *lows* by the Saxons, and bearing no relation in modern English to their location!

The places where the Saxons established settlements often contain the element *inga*, as in Hartington. The common suffix *ley* indicates where the woodland was cleared, and other words such as as clough, den, shaw, and hirst — relating either to clearings or to the presence of old woodland — show the wide extent of the Saxon clearance and colonisation.

In comparison, there is little Danish or Viking influence in the place names of the Peak. The Danish *hulm*, meaning island or water meadow, appears in the south-west and *by* was their word for town. A few places bear the name of pagan Scandinavian deities and Winster, Wensley, and Edensor are thought to originate from Woden, the god of war. This relative paucity indicates the Peak's intermediate position between the Danelaw to the east and the Norse stronghold to the north-west.

Most names were established by Domesday but, during the Middle Ages, a few individual settlements came to be known as granges. These were sheep farms, situated mainly on the limestone, attached to one of the great monastic institutions. Later still, the enclosure of earlier waste land created new farms and such areas were called 'intake'. There is an 'Intake Farm' just north of Little Hucklow, and further instances of the name on the steep western slope of the eastern moors.

The 'black river' — the River Dove

Great mullein (above) and campion (below) can be found on the southern bank of Lathkill Dale.

Teal can be found breeding on the large artificial reservoirs.

Woodland

There is little natural woodland left on the gritstone but patches occur in less accessible rocky cloughs and in Padley Gorge and Ladybower and Priddock Woods. These valuable sites are now carefully managed and are dominated by sessile oak — so called because the acorns have no stalk — and birch, with alder in the wetter ground beside streams. Bilberry and wavy hair grass dominate the woodland floor with occasional ferns such as the broad buckler and the hard fern.

An interesting feature is formed by the heaps of earth constructed by the aggressive wood ants. Insects, in fact, are especially numerous and varied for oaks can support nearly 300 species. This naturally attracts a great variety of birds including woodpeckers, tits, tree creepers, warblers, redstarts, and nuthatches. Nestboxes established in Padley Gorge have encour-

aged the pied flycatcher, here at the limit of its range. The fringes of the woodland are home for the rare nightjar and black grouse but don't ask any official for the location!

Unfortunately, the area occupied by deciduous woodland is far exceeded by that devoted to softwoods. The upper Derwent, in particular, is heavily cloaked in dark conifer plantations which are comparatively poor in species, but they do attract some interesting birds and animals including sparrowhawks, goldcrests, siskins and crossbills. Goshawks and red squirrels are among the rarer inhabitants.

Limestone country

The limestone forms much lighter, open scenery and, because it escaped glaciation during the last Ice Age, it has developed a rich alkaline soil that supports a tremendous variety of plants and animals. The uplands are now largely given over to improved pasture but, before enclosure in the seventeenth and eighteenth centuries, they were covered mainly in heathland. Most fields are seeded with a few modern species that are cut regularly for silage and support few types of plants. The stone walls, though, are home to vole and shrew, and to nesting wheatears and stonechats. Where the pastures are unimproved, though, there are many more species including meadow saxifrage, cowslip, marjoram, thyme, harebell, orchids, rock rose, and bird's-foot trefoil. There can be up to fifty-four species in a square metre of such grassland, and the Park actively encourages farmers to preserve these old meadows.

The ground is abuzz and alive with insects in summer. Most noticeable are the butterflies which include the brown argus, the green hairstreak, the orange tip and the common blue. The slowworm can also be found on the warm southern slopes. Soaring above these are lapwings, skylarks, and meadow pipits although these are scarcer where their nests are disturbed by regular silage cutting. In winter there are visits from fieldfares and redwings.

Artificial habitats

Surprisingly, some of the richest habitats are entirely artificial, and an interesting set of flora exists on the old lead mine workings, many of which have lain undisturbed for centuries. The spring sandwort, known locally as leadwort, specialises in such sites, and miners could detect lead veins by locating the five delicate white stars of the flowers which appear in early summer. It can withstand unusually high levels of lead and is otherwise very rare. On less toxic parts of the waste heaps grows the yellow mountain pansy, eyebright, and autumn gentians.

The creation of trails through old railway cuttings and embankments has also provided a fertile environment, and the keen eyed will spot bloody cranesbill — locally called 'thunderclouds' because it flowers in the thundery days of July — kidney vetch and even the rare Nottingham Catchfly.

The dales are the Peak's outstanding wildlife resource and many are managed and protected by the Nature Conservancy Council, the National Trust, and the Derbyshire Wildlife Trust. Their natural vegetation is woodland but much of this was removed during the Middle Ages and for later lead mining activities. Many limestone woods were planted during the last century with species such as beech and sycamore. There is a variety of trees with ash being the dominant among a collection that includes elm, hazel, and hawthorn. In the older woods such as those in Dovedale and the southern bank of Lathkill Dale, there is also yew, bird cherry, field maple, and buckthorn. The floor is carpeted with a delightful array of colourful flowers such as campion, herb Robert, wood anemone, mullein, ramsons, bluebells, and yellow archangel. It is also home to the purple mezereon — nationally a rare plant. Flitting among the trees are chaffinches, woodpeckers, wood and willow warblers, spotted flycatchers, and chiff-chaffs.

The rocky outcrops on the dale sides form another distinct habitat reflected in their unusual flora. They are particularly valuable sites because their inaccessibility to people and to grazing animals has left them largely undisturbed. The dry rock is favoured by lichens, mosses, and stonewort. Ferns inhabit the shady cracks and include maidenhair spleenwort, wall rue, hart's-tongue fern, and the rare and beautiful limestone fern. There are a few trees, such as ash and yew, but water and anchorage are considerable problems. In summer some of the damp dale bottoms contain clumps of Jacob's Ladder — another rare Peakland speciality — with its deep blue flowers and distinctive yellow stamens.

The water courses are are also full of life, including species such as crayfish which will only inhabit the cleanest waters. Streams like the Lathkill and the Bradford that rise wholly or partly on limestone are among the purest in Britain, and are nationally renowned for their trout. Feeding on the numerous fish, dragonflies, and other insects is a variety of birds including kingfisher, dippers, and pied and grey wagtails. A different type of waterlife is found on the large artificial reservoirs but the range of species is nowhere near as great. Teal and common sandpiper breed on these sites but otherwise the reservoirs are used as seasonal homes by migrant birds such as pochard, goldeneye, and goosander.

The Peak offers a wealth of possibilities for the dedicated naturalist because of the exceptional variety of habitats that lie in close proximity to one another. The environment, though, is fragile — dependent on an intricate and delicate relationship between people, land and climate. The future of the unique and precious landscapes of the Peak will depend on how the varying demands made on the area's resources are balanced and managed.

The combination of farmland, woodland and moors offers the dedicated naturalist many possibilities.

Leisure Activities

Useful Names & Addresses

More information is available from Tourist Information Centres, along with information about accommodation.

Tourist Information Centres
Bakewell: (062 981) 3227 *
Buxton: (0298) 5106 *
Castleton: (0433) 20679
Edale: (0433) 70207 *
Glossop: (04574) 5920
Matlock Bath: (0629) 55082

*run by the Peak Park Joint Planning Board who produce useful 'Fact Finder' leaflets on sport and leisure activities within the Park. Head office: Aldern House, Baslow Road, Bakewell, Derbyshire DE4 1AE (062 981) 4321. They also produce a 'Fact Finder' leaflet containing information on facilities for the disabled in the Peak Park.

TRANSPORT

Buses
East Midland Bus Company (0246) 211007
Trent Bus Company (0332) 43201
Chesterfield Transport (0246) 207103
South Yorkshire Bus Company (0742) 755655
Potteries Motor Transport (0782) 747000
Silver Service — for buses operating within the Peak (0629) 580212 Hulleys — Baslow (024 688) 2246

Trains
British Rail Enquiries:
Alfreton (0602) 476151
Buxton (0298) 22101
Chesterfield (0742) 726411
Derby (0332) 32051
Glossop (045 74) 2285
Nottingham (0602) 476151
Sheffield (0742) 726411

Mountain Rescue and Cave Rescue
Any area — dial 999 and ask for mountain/cave rescue

LEISURE ACTIVITIES

Canal Trips
Cromford Canal — Horse-drawn trip from Cromford Wharf (062 982) 3727

Canoeing
The British Canoe Union (0602) 691944, Derwent area advisor (033 17) 4972
Matlock Canoe Club (0629) 55046

Camping and Caravanning
A comprehensive list of caravan and campsites is produced annually by the Park, obtainable at Tourist Information Centres

Site availability from Caravan Advisory Service (0629) 814341 (24 hours). Cheap and basic accommodation is available in camping barns. Information from Tourist Information Centres but book through Losehill Hall (0433) 20373.

Camping and Caravanning Club (071) 828 1012/6

Caravan Club (0342) 26944

Caving
The Derbyshire Caving Association (0602) 821887/822586. The National Caving Association 021 472 1301
The Peak District Mines Historical Society (0629) 3834

Cycle Hire
Derwent Cycle Hire, Fairholmes, (110) SK 173893, Tel: (0335) 43156. Parsley Hay Cycle Hire: (Tissington and High Peak Trails), Tel:(0298) 84493, (119) SK 146637. Waterhouses Cycle Hire: (Manifold Trail), Tel: (0538) 308609, (119) SK 085501, Middleton Top. (High Peak Trail) Tel: (0629) 823204, (119) SK 276552, Hayfield: (Sett Valley Trail), Tel: (0663) 46222, (110) SK 036869, Lyme Park: Disley Tel: (066 32) 2032
A. J. & M. Sears, Hartington; Tel: Hartington (029 884) 459. Monsal Head Cycle Hire, Tel: Great Longstone (062 987) 505

Fishing
National Anglers Council (0733) 54084
National Federation of Anglers (0332) 362000
Severn Trent Water Authority (021) 722 4000
Yorkshire Water (0532) 440191
North West Water Authority (0925) 53999

Gliding
The Derbyshire and Lancashire Gliding Club (Great Hucklow): Buxton (0298) 871270. Staffordshire Gliding Club (Morridge): Sheffield (0742) 668597

Golf
Bakewell Golf Club (062981) 2307
Buxton and High Peak Club (0298) 26263
Cavendish Golf Club — Buxton (0298) 23494
Chapel-en-le-Frith (0298) 812118
Glossop (04574) 64275
Matlock Golf Club (0629) 582191

Sickle Holme — Bamford (0433) 51506

Hang Gliding
Peak District Flight Training (0538) 383659
Peak School of Hang Gliding (0283) 43879

Riding Stables
Buxton Riding School (0298) 72319
Curbar Edge School (0433) 550049
Hargate Hill Riding Centre, Glossop (045 74) 65518
Hopkin Farm, Matlock (0629) 2253
Lady Booth, Edale (0433) 70205
Northfield Farm, Flash (0298) 2543
Red House Stables, Matlock (0629) 733583
Rushup Hall, Chapel-en-le-Frith (0298) 3323

Sailing
Dovestones Sailing Club (Dovestones Reservoir) (0422) 882908. Errwood Sailing Club. Glossop and District Sailing Club (Torside Reservoir) (061 338) 4764. Sheffield Viking Sailing Club (Damflask Reservoir) (0742) 351577.

Sports Centres
Glossop Leisure Centre (045 74) 63223. Sherwood Hall Sports and Leisure Centre — Matlock (0629) 56111.

Squash Courts
Cressbrook Mill (0298) 871228
Glossop Leisure Centre (045 74) 63223
Wirksworth (062 982) 3364

Swimming
Buxton Spa (0298) 6548
Glossop (045 74) 4365
Hathersage Open Air (0433) 50843
Matlock Lido (0629) 582843

Walks
Walking guide books and leaflets, and information about guided walks can be obtained from the National Park Information Centres.

Youth Hostels
The first number listed is the telephone number, then the number of the 1:50,000 map followed by the grid reference. * denotes a hostel run by the Peak Park Joint Planning Board, open to all members of the public. † by Nottinghamshire Education Authority.

Bakewell: Bakewell 2313; (119) 215685.
Bretton: Sheffield 884541; (119) 200780.
Buxton: Buxton 2287; (119) 062722.
Castleton: Hope Valley 20235; (110) 150828.
Crowden-in-Longendale*: Glossop 2135; (110) 073993.
Edale: Hope Valley 70302; (110) 139865.
Elton: Winster 394; (119) 224608.
Eyam: Hope Valley 30335; (119) 219769.
Gradbach Mill: Wincle 625; (118) 993661.
Hagg Farm†: Hope Valley 51594; (110) 161888
Hartington: Hartington 223; (119) 131603.
Hathersage: Hope Valley 50493; (110) 226814.
Ilam Hall: Thorpe Cloud 212; (119) 131506.
Langsett: Barnsley 762445; (110) 211005
Matlock: Matlock 2983; (119) 300603
Meerbrook: Blackshaw 244; (118) 989608.
Ravenstor: Tideswell 871826; (119) 152732.
Youlegreave: Youlegreave 518; (119) 210641.

More information from: Youth Hostels Association, National Office, Trevelyan House, 8 St Stephen's Hill, St Albans, Herts Al1 2DY (St Albans 55215).

Gliding at Great Hucklow.

Places of interest

Stars (★) after a place name indicate that the place is featured elsewhere in this section.

Alport
(119) (SK 2264) ³/₄ mile E of Youlgreave
Alport is a delightful small village situated at the confluence of the Lathkill and Bradford Rivers. In the past it made good industrial use of the available water power, and a mill and mill pool still survive. With the surrounding water meadows, its seventeenth- and eighteenth-century cottages, and ancient bridge, it is a very attractive spot popular with artists. Alport is included on **Walk 1**.

Limestone crags beside the River Bradford near Alport.

Alport Castles
(110) (SK 1491) 3 miles N of Edale
Not to be linked with the village of Alport, this impressive feature lies in remote countryside above Alport Dale, west of the Derwent Reservoir. As at Mock Beggar Hall (Robin Hood's Stride) ★ , the natural array of towers and pinnacles has been likened to some construction by human hands. In this case, they are thought to resemble ruined fortifications and the 'Tower' is a pinnacle of rock that has become separated from the plateau behind it by a spectacular landslip said to be one of the largest in Britain. It is part of a mass nearly ¹/₂ mile long that has dropped about 100 feet below the main cliff. It may seem improbable today that the cause of the instability was the tiny River Alport which undermined the gritstone by cutting into the soft shales beneath. This occurred during the much wetter climate after the Ice Age when the volume of water in the river would have been greatly increased. Alport Castles are included on **Walk 5**.

Wetton Hill near Alstonefield.

Alstonefield
(119) (SK 1355) 3¹/₂ miles S of Hartington
Situated on high ground between the Rivers Dove and Manifold, Alstonefield was ignored by the canal and railway barons and remains today a largely unspoilt village. The green is surrounded by a cluster of attractive buildings including the Hall, dated 1587, and the popular George Inn. The earliest parts of the church are Norman but it was built over successive centu-

The impressive Alport Castles.

Sheepwash Bridge — one of several bridges in Ashford in the Water.

ries and also contains Decorated and Perpendicular work. Inside there are many fine seventeenth-century artefacts including a double-decker pulpit and carved oak box pews. One of these belonged to Charles Cotton, friend of Izaak Walton and co-author of *The Compleat Angler*. Although living closer to Hartington ★ at Beresford Hall, he had close associations with the village. Alstonefield is visited on **Tour 9**.

Arbor Low (119) (SK 1663) 2 miles S of Monyash
This is the Peak's major prehistoric monument, cared for by English Heritage and of such importance as to have been dubbed 'The Stonehenge of the North'. This may not be at first apparent, for the stones lie flat as if pushed over by some gigantic hand. It is probable that the stones were upright when the henge was originally constructed around 2000 BC. The forty-six slabs of limestone form a 150-foot circle and surround an inner set of four, the whole contained within a roughly circular bank and ditch extending over 250 feet in diameter. It occupies an exposed site at 1230 feet on a windswept ridge, reached by a concessionary route from the road along the track to Upper Oldhams Farm. It is surrounded by other 'lows' whose origins and functions are just as obscure. It was obviously

an important site, for connected to the henge and just 350 yards to the south-west lies Gib Hill, another Bronze Age barrow which had itself been built over an earlier Neolithic cairn.

Ashford in the Water (119) (SK 1969) 1½ miles NW of Bakewell
Ashford is sited at an important crossing point over the River Wye and lies on the route of the ancient Portway, one of the Peak District's oldest tracks. There are several bridges in the village but the one that most catches the eye is the medieval Sheepwash Bridge, named from the adjacent stone pen where sheep were kept before being washed in the river. The village once rivalled Bakewell ★ and, in the seventeenth century, 300 packhorses, mostly carrying malt, passed through each week. Later on, a stocking industry became established and, by the early nineteenth century, there were up to eighty frames working in the village. **Tours 1 and 3** pass through Ashford and it is recommended that the visitor takes extra time to explore the nooks and crannies, and to stroll among its attractive buildings.

Apart from the bridges, there are numerous eighteenth-century buildings, and inside the church are examples of the local Ashford Marble, including a beautifully inlaid table. Above the aisles hang four garlands known as 'virgin crants',

Fine examples of Ashford Marble can be found inside the church.

once carried at the funerals of unmarried girls and later hung over the family pews. The last crant was carried in 1801. The village wake begins every year on Trinity Sunday to celebrate the church's founding and to dress six village wells as a thanksgiving for the precious supply of spring water.

Axe Edge (118 and 119) (SK 0370 — highest point) Extends SW of Buxton

As will be appreciated on **Tour 7**, there are very good views from the A53, which runs along the eastern edge of the escarpment. To the east lies rolling White Peak scenery, while to the west the darker heather-covered moorland betrays the underlying gritstone. The land rises to 1807 feet and nearby are some of the country's highest hostelries, including The Cat and Fiddle Inn which, at 1690 feet, claims to be the second highest pub in Britain. It can be a bleak place, receiving over 50 inches of rain a year, which would seem to make it a fitting source for five of the region's major rivers. To the east rise the Dove and the Manifold, initially following closely parallel courses. The Wye rises just to the north above Buxton ★ while to the west lie the sources of the Dane and the Goyt, the latter destined to become a major source for the River Mersey.

Bakewell (119) (SK 2168)

Bakewell is popularly regarded as the 'capital' of the Peak District, being not only the largest town within the National Park, but also headquarters of the Peak Park Joint Planning Board. It has a busy Monday market and is renowned for its one-day agricultural show held in August. Bakewell was a crossing point over the Wye but would also have been an important site for its water supply, as its original name 'Badeca's Waelle' implies. It is known that in 942 Edward the Elder ordered the construction and manning of a fort near the town, but the site has not yet been positively identified.

The Saxons have left more durable evidence of their passing in the damaged but still impressive 8-foot high eighth-century cross shaft in the churchyard. It has not always stood here for, although the church site is thought to be ancient, the cross itself was brought in from the surrounding country where it may have been used as a wayside preaching cross. Near the south porch is a smaller cross stump, thought to be tenth century, while just inside the porch there are many Saxon fragments among the fascinating collection of carved stones. A few elements of the Saxon church remain but the building is composed of a mixture of styles from Norman to Victorian, the latter period respon-

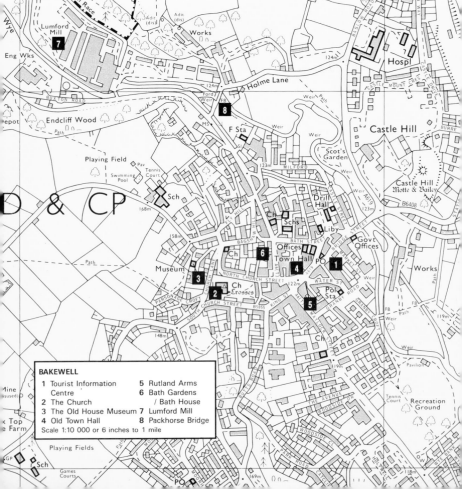

BAKEWELL

1 Tourist Information
  Centre
2 The Church
3 The Old House Museum
4 Old Town Hall

5 Rutland Arms
6 Bath Gardens
  / Bath House
7 Lumford Mill
8 Packhorse Bridge

Scale 1:10 000 or 6 inches to 1 mile

Above: *some fine Saxon carvings can be found inside Bakewell church.* Right: *the church is dominated by its Victorian tower and spire.*

sible for the dominating tower and spire.

Inside is a number of medieval monuments, including that of Dorothy Vernon and John Manners, who are said to have eloped from nearby Haddon Hall ★ . Just up the hill from the church, the Old House Museum is housed in a sixteenth-century Tudor building. It has been conserved and restored by Bakewell Historical Society and still contains its original wattle and daub interior walls. Inside is an interesting display of local history and industrial archaeology. Just below the church is the old Town Hall of 1684, with a row of early eighteenth-century almshouses behind. Down in the town itself are a number of fine old buildings. The Park's main Information Centre is housed in the seventeenth-century market hall, while nearby Rutland Square was set out in 1804, when the Rutland Arms was built — scene of the disaster that led to the first Bakewell pudding. Just opposite are Bath Gardens and Bath House, built over a natural spring by the Duke of Rutland in 1697 in an unsuccessful attempt to encourage the growth of a spa. He failed because the water was colder than that at Buxton ★ .

To the north of the town lies Lumford Mill, established by Arkwright in 1777. Spanning the Wye nearby there is an attractive packhorse bridge of 1664 with its typical low parapets to aid the crossing. The main town bridge preceded it by over 300 years but has obviously undergone considerable alteration since, including widening in the nineteenth century. Bakewell is included in **Tours 1**, **3**, and **8**, and a stroll is highly recommended. The paths beside the river near the town bridge are particularly pleasant.

Bamford (110) (SK 2083) 2 miles NW of Hathersage

Although its railway station lies somewhat inconveniently on the Hope Valley line, Bamford itself lies beneath a gritstone edge beside the Derwent. The cotton mill dates from around 1792 and finally closed in 1965. However, it has retained its 30-foot by 22-foot waterwheel and a 1907 tandem compound steam engine, which is steamed on open days. The church was built in 1861 just after Bamford became an independent parish. It is a William Butterfield design, unusual for Derbyshire with its slender tower and

spire. Bamford is also known for its annual sheep dog trials and its site as the last village before the Derwent reservoirs to the north. It is visited on **Tours 3** and **10**.

Baslow (119) (SK 2572) 3¼ miles NE of Bakewell

There are three distinct parts to the village, which grew up at the site where the Sheffield and Chesterfield roads cross the Derwent. At Bridge End, on the northern edge of the village, the attractive three-arched stone bridge dates from 1603 and is reputedly the only bridge across the Derwent never to have been destroyed by floods. The diminutive watchman's hut was used by villagers to collect tolls and control traffic over the bridge. They were certainly no race of giants but the tiny doorway may have been subsequently reduced by road repairs. The east dial of the clock on the church spire was designed by the army surgeon Dr Wrench and displays 'VICTORIA 1897' instead of numerals in celebration of Queen Victoria's Diamond Jubilee. Inside is a leather dog whip used to clear stray dogs from the church during services. Baslow is located at the northern end

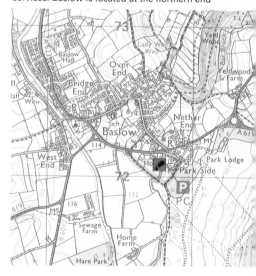

BEELEY

Eagle Stone on Baslow Edge.

of Chatsworth ★ Park and, indeed, seems to possess something of a stately air itself with some impressive buildings such as the Cavendish Hotel. After the roads were improved, the village became popular with the more wealthy from the nearby towns and cities who came to enjoy the country air and visit Chatsworth. Many guesthouses were opened and, in 1881, a hydropathic hotel was built, sadly pulled down in 1936.

Baslow is included on **Tours 3** and **9**. The car park beside the A619 is a good place to start a stroll around the village. Above the village on Baslow Edge stands the Wellington Monument, visited on **Walk 3**. It was erected in 1866 by Dr Wrench who, as an army man, felt the need to counterbalance the memorial dedicated to Admiral Nelson on nearby Birchen Edge.

Beeley (119) (SK 2667) 3 miles E of Bakewell
Beeley lies at the southern end of Chatsworth ★ Park and remains an estate village, laid out mostly by Paxton for the Sixth Duke of Devonshire. **Tour 9** passes through the village but it is easy to miss the main street, which lies

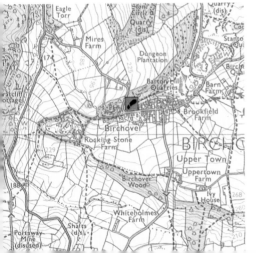

to the east of the major road to Chatsworth. Some buildings are older, including the seventeenth-century Hall where Charles Dickens was wont to stay. Beeley Moor above the village contains an abundance of ancient barrows and cairns. Hob Hurst's House is a Bronze Age barrow named from the mischievous wood elf 'Hob i' th' Hurst'. Bateman found a pile of burnt human bones here in his excavation of 1853.

Birchover (119) (SK 2362) 1 mile north of Winster
Recorded in Domesday as 'Barcovere', its name literally means 'at the birch-covered steep slope'. The substantial quarry at the upper end of Birchover quarries the pinkish tinged gritstone from which much of this attractive solid village is constructed. The Druid Inn is the better known of the two pubs, renowned for the choice and quality of the bar food. The pub's name was influenced by the proximity of Rowtor Rocks — an exposed gritstone outcrop just behind the Inn once thought to be a place of pagan Druid worship. There is a concessionary path through the rocks and, once on top, it can be seen that they are part of an east-west ridge. Although they rise no more than 150 feet and extend just 80 yards, their weird, contorted shapes make an impressive spectacle. The views are good, too, to the north and west, taking in parts of Youlgreave ★ , Cratcliffe Tor, and the unmistakable wobbly towers of Robin Hood's Stride ★ .

The steps, seats and caves are the work of the somewhat eccentric Reverend Thomas Eyre, who lived at nearby Rowtor Hall and died in 1717. He cut the seats for his friends but he himself liked to sit among the rocks and compose sermons. If you are tempted to explore, be careful in wet weather because the rocks are covered in moss and can be very slippery. There does seem to be an air of mystery about Birchover. Perhaps it is the Druid connection or possibly the numerous archaeological sites close to the village. There are prehistoric monuments on Harthill Moor to the west, while Stanton Moor to the east was clearly a very important place for burial and worship, having yielded at least seventy Bronze Age barrows. Some of these can be seen from **Walk 10**.

Black Hill (110) (SK 0704) 7 Miles NE of Glossop
Wainwright did not care very much for these hills of the northern Peak. He did not seem to have a kind word for Bleaklow ★ and described Black Hill as a 'desolate and hopeless quagmire'. Little grows here beside the peat and he continued: 'Nature fashioned it but for once has no suggestion for clothing it'. Each visitor must form his or her own opinion but there is a beauty in the barren untamed moor which offers space and wide skies for those prepared to explore its wilderness. The land is not left entirely to its own devices, for the high moors of the northern Peak are managed for grouse, and here and there are numerous grouse shooting cabins. Walkers may be suddenly disturbed by a rising bird with its cry of 'go back, go back'.

Situated in the far north of the Park, Black Hill reaches 1,908 feet. The summit is broad, flat,

and usually waterlogged with the intriguing name of Soldier's Lump. This refers to the military surveys that have taken place here. In 1841, the wooden framework used for a survey in 1784 was discovered on the site now occupied by the concrete pillar. This supported one of Ramsden's famous theodolites, now exhibited in the Science Museum. To the east is the well-known 740-foot high needle of the BBC's Holme Moss television transmitter. This replaces the original mast which, when erected in 1951, was then the most powerful TV transmitter in the world.

Black Hill has had its quota of drama and disaster. Just below Chew Reservoir to the south-west — incidentally one of the highest in the country at 1600 feet — the Chew Brook flows through a dramatic galley which was the scene of an avalanche in 1963 that killed two experienced climbers. In 1949 a Dakota aircraft crashed on nearby Wimberry Rocks killing the crew and twenty-four passengers, while the land to the north of the summit was the site of the Moors Murders. Most people, of course, visit the area without incident. The Pennine Way approaches the hill from Edale ★ to the south on two alternative paths. The original route offered direct and safe access to the summit via Hey Edge but, since 1966, the official path lies further west through Laddow Rocks. Similarly, the Way leaves the hill on two alternative routes. The main path runs over White Moss, cut east-west by the Cotton Famine Road dug by unemployed cotton workers desperate for work and food. Now only a ditch remains to mark their labours. The other path descends into the Wessenden Valley and beside the reservoirs of the Shiny Brook.

The unmistakable towers of Robin Hood's Stride near Birchover.

28 feet lower than Kinder Scout ★, yet receives far fewer visitors than its better-known southern neighbour. It seems impossible that anything could survive on the dark acid peat, and Bleaklow has earned the description of Britain's only true desert. In this case, it is a cold desert in which the black hags and groughs of peat are relieved only intermittently by cotton or hare's tail grass. Even Alfred Wainwright, who devoted much of his life exploring the British fells, was wont to say that 'Nobody loves Bleaklow....All who get on it are glad to get off'. Prospective walkers should be warned by the names on the map — Black Clough, Coldharbour Moor, The Swamp. And yet the plateau has an untamed beauty and offers a chance of that true solitude that is so rare to find today.

The scenery is not empty of interest. The tors of Bleaklow have shapes as fascinating as their names. The Grinah Stones have a curious pockmarked appearance and offer superb views over to Derwent Edge. The Anvil Stone and the Trident, part of the group known as Bleaklow Stones, are well named, while the Wain Stones resemble a kissing couple. The Barrow Stones are another interesting group and overlook the source of the River Derwent at Swains Greave.

Tors are not the only features of the plateau nor is every visitor a keen walker. Some may be aviation historians seeking out the not infrequent wrecks of aircraft that came to grief on the hill. Many date from World War II and, among the largest is an American Super Fortress lying not far from Bleaklow Head

---

Bleaklow (110) (SK 0995) 4 miles NE of Glossop
Many would think the modern spelling of the Old English *blaec hlaw* — 'dark-coloured hill' — to be most appropriate for this wet, barren wilderness. The plateau lies at over 2000 feet, only

Bonsall (119) (SK 2758) 1 mile E of Matlock Bath
It is necessary to exert a little energy to explore this village for it rises 450 feet almost to the top of the limestone plateau. About half way up in the market place is a striking medieval cross

45

atop a nineteenth-century shaft and a circular base of thirteen stone steps. It is surrounded by attractive limestone buildings, including the King's Head, established in 1677. Stockings were made here but the village was principally a lead-mining centre. The Bonsall Brook rises on the upland and flows south-eastwards towards Cromford ★ , where it proved significant in Arkwright's choice of site for his mill. The village dresses at least three wells, using only natural materials, usually in late July.

Bradfield (110) (SK 2692) 6³/₄ miles NW of Bamford
Bradfield Dale is one of the least visited of the larger valleys in the Peak District. This is not surprising because the surrounding gritstone moorlands isolate it from the more popular areas to the west and south. Lying in South Yorkshire, it is best known by Sheffield folk, who also drink the water supplied by the string of reservoirs constructed along the River Loxley.

The village is divided into two, and Low Bradfield is peaceful enough today with its cottages and farm buildings surrounding the cricket field. In 1864, however, it was the scene of Britain's greatest dam disaster with the failure of the 1200-foot long and 100-foot high dam holding up Dale Dike Reservoir. Water surged down the valley destroying fifteen bridges, decimating over 600 buildings, and killing 240 people. The new dam was built in 1875 and so far has proved more adequate for the task. Upper Bradfield occupies a splendid position. The view from the south porch of the church across the valley and reservoirs to the moors beyond must be one of the best to be had from any churchyard in the country. The church itself is surprisingly grand for a small village but was built largely by Ecclesfield Priory, which also supplied the first clergymen. The building is remarkable for its highly embattled fourteenth-century tower, its pinnacles, and its array of gargoyles. There are also some elements of Norman work but it dates chiefly from the fifteenth century.

The curiously shaped house next to the church is the Watch House, one of very few remaining in Britain. It was built in 1745 at a time when body snatching was rife and was used to guard against any intruders into the nearby graveyard. Just to the north-west of the church is a 58-foot high mound, part of the remains of a Norman

One of the areas famous dressed wells at Bradwell.

motte and bailey castle. Castle Hill to the east of the village is another earthwork, where a small tower may have stood. There is a lot to see here for such a small village and the visitor is recommended to take a stroll and study it at leisure. It is visited on **Tour 5**.

Bradwell (110) (SK 1781) 2 miles SE of Castleton
Bradwell lies at the northern end of Bradwell Dale where it broadens out to meet the Hope Valley. It has had a busy, largely industrial history, initially important as a lead mining centre. It became famous for the manufacture of hard lead miner's hats called 'Bradder beavers' but it is now better known for the huge cement works on its western edge. Perhaps more happily, it is also renowned for its homemade ice cream and the Bagshawe show cavern. This ¹/₂-mile cave was discovered in 1806 and is reached by descending 100 or so steps through an old lead mine. Its past and present activities have given Bradwell a workaday appearance but the village has lots of character. It is included on **Tour 10**.

Brassington (119) (SK 2354) 3¹/₂ miles west of Wirksworth
Brassington lies just outside the south-eastern boundary of the National Park but in appearance looks like a typical Peakland limestone hill village. It is a very attractive old lead mining village and examples of the vernacular cottage architecture abound — including a particularly fine building of 1615, complete with stone mullioned windows. There has been considerable recent development but, on the whole, it has used sympathetic materials and blends in well with the older parts of the village. The tower and a considerable portion of the rest of the church is Norman. Of even greater age, though, is the Saxon carving of a man with his hand on his heart situated high up in the west

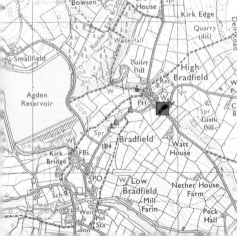

BUXTON

1 Tourist Information
   Centre
2 The Crescent
3 Library (ceiling)
4 Royal Devonshire
   Hospital

5 Pavilion / Pavilion
   Gardens
6 Opera House
7 Palace Hotel
8 The Micrarium
9 Peak Railway Centre
   (Buxton Steam Centre)

Scale 1:10 000 or 6 inches to 1 mile

wall of the tower. The figure is ³/₄ length on a stone measuring 12 inches by 10 inches and requires a little persistence to locate.

A mile to the north-west are the curious rocks and cave of Harboro' Rocks. Excavations in 1907 and 1923 yielded animal remains of the Old Stone Age, and finds of pottery and brooches indicate that the cave was inhabited at least from the Iron Age and probably earlier. Its long history of occupation probably continued to medieval times, and Daniel Defoe, on his travels in the eighteenth century, discovered a family of six living here. There is an excellent viewpoint from the summit, which is occupied by both a triangulation point and a Neolithic tomb, dating from around 2500 BC. This was obviously a site of some importance, also lying just ¹/₂ mile west of the ancient Portway.

Of considerably more recent vintage are the font, chair, and pulpit that have been shaped out of the rock. Brassington is included on **Tour 2**.

Buxton (119) (SK 0673)

Buxton grew up as a spa town, and remains the chief resort of the Peak. Its grand and impressive architecture and its entertainment and accommodation facilities have no rival elsewhere. Despite this, it was excluded from the National Park but the explanation is not hard to find for, as will become clear from **Tours 4**, **6**, and **7**, the town is ringed by scarred landscapes resulting from intensive limestone quarrying. There is much to see in Buxton, however, and no visit to the Peak District would be complete without a look at the town. Take an extra layer of clothing, though, for at 1000 feet (it is said to be the highest town in England), it is at least a topcoat colder than most other places in the Peak.

Not that this seemed to bother the Romans, who found the warm mineral water issuing from eight thermal springs very attractive. Buxton is sited where water is forced upwards at the junction of the limestone and the shale and grit. It

Growing up as a spa town, Buxton boasts many grand buildings and parks, amongst which are the Crescent (above), and the Pavilion Gardens (right).

comes from depths as great as 5000 feet and up to a quarter of a million gallons emerge daily at a constant temperature of 82 °F. The Romans built a bath and a network of roads converged on the settlement. The water became known for its health-giving properties and has continued to attract the sick and infirm. Many famous people have visited the springs including Mary Queen of Scots, who found relief for her rheumatism. You can sample the water for yourself at St Ann's Well, opposite the Tourist Information Centre.

The original settlement grew on the higher ground on the limestone and is rather different in appearance and character to the more famous development lower down. This latter grew from the desire of the Fifth Duke of Devonshire to establish a spa town to rival Bath. He commissioned John Carr of York to design a Crescent along the lines of the structure at Bath. This magnificent Doric-style building was completed in 1784 and originally housed three hotels. The library now occupies the site of the Great Hotel and should be visited if only to view the ceiling. The Duke next built the Stables in 1785-90, later converted to the Royal Devonshire Hospital in 1859. The central dome was built in 1881 and, with a diameter of 156 feet and a weight of 560 tons, it remained for a long time the largest unsupported dome in the world.

Buxton rapidly became fashionable and the Sixth Duke appointed Sir John Wyatville to design the elegant classical church of St John the Baptist and the paths of The Slopes. In the mid-nineteenth century, Paxton was responsible for the development of The Park and the houses overlooking it. The coming of the railway in 1863 marked the peak of Buxton's popularity, prompting further grand building projects such as the Palace Hotel in 1868, the Pavilion and Pavilion Gardens in 1871, and the imposing Opera House in 1905. The town declined in the twentieth century but has recently revived somewhat with a growing reputation as a cultural centre. The annual Festival of Music and the Arts is nationally important. Some of the buildings have been refurbished and restored, and the A6 now bypasses the town.

Other features of note include the Micrarium, housed in the old Pump Room, with a fascinat-

ing collection of exhibits to be viewed under microscopes. Near the old railway station, the Peak Railway Centre has four working locomotives and others undergoing restoration. In the upper town are the interesting Museum and Art gallery and the unusual seventeenth-century chapel of St Anne. There is so much to see in Buxton that it is recommended that several hours are allocated for a stroll around the town. There are also several places of interest just to the south of the town. Poole's Cavern is a natural cave and source of the River Wye. It was used by early humans and was one of the 'First Wonders' of the Peak. Grin Low Woods have been designated a country park and there are some rare flora in its 100 acres. A short walk away is Solomon's Temple, built as a folly in 1896 on top of a Neolithic tumulus. At a height of 1440 feet, it commands excellent views of Buxton and the surrounding area.

Calver (119) (SK 2474) 1½ miles NW of Baslow
Calver was sited at a crossing point over the Derwent. It still retains a fine eighteenth-cen-

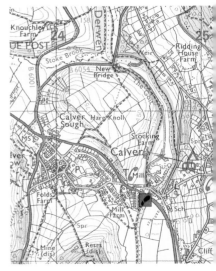

tury stone bridge, which has been bypassed to the west by the A623. Nearby is an imposing former textile mill, built by Arkwright in 1803-4 and put to use in recent times as the setting for the TV series *Colditz*. To the west, the settlement of Calver Sough is a reminder of former lead mining days, deriving its name from a drainage sough from an old lead mine last worked in the middle of the nineteenth century. There is a pleasant stroll beside the Derwent leading north from Calver Bridge and returning down the east bank. The village is included on **Tours 3** and **9**.

Castleton (110) (SK 1583) 1½ miles W of Hope Castleton is a busy tourist centre with many attractions to occupy the visitor. The most famous of these are the show caves but the most visible is the keep of Peveril Castle, dominating the town from its perch of limestone. With steep drops on three sides and a high stone wall on the fourth, the castle was virtually

The imposing former textile mill at Calver.

The keep of Peveril Castle is one of Castleton's most visible attractions.

impregnable. It was built by William Peveril, an illegitimate son of William the Conqueror, and its Domesday entry of 1086 indicates it to be one of the first stone-built castles in the country. Henry II repossessed the castle from the Peverils and it was he who built the 60-foot high tower in 1176.

Castleton gained an early importance as the administrative centre of the Royal Forest of the Peak, but the siting of the castle may also have been determined by the need to protect the valuable lead mines of the area. Whatever the reason, the settlement grew up close to the protection of the castle walls and was aptly named 'Castle Town'. The development was not haphazard, though, and from higher ground, it is possible to determine that the layout of the village was carefully planned so that castle and village could be defended together. The present town, however, does not occupy the original pre-Norman site, which was in a more favourable position on Treak Cliff out of the path of the prevailing wind.

Castleton occupies a wonderful setting rich in geographical and geological interest. It is sited at the junction of the limestone and the grits and shales, and surrounded on three sides by dramatic hills, caves, and gorges. To the north is the distinctive Mam Tor-Lose Hill ridge, separating the Hope Valley from the Vale of Edale. Mam Tor ★ rises to 1695 feet, and the exposed striped face reveals its layers of soft shale and harder grits that are the cause of its instability. It is also known as the 'Shivering Mountain' and a landslip in 1977 swept away the A625 at the foot of the hill. The old road can be seen from the top of the ridge on **Walk 4** which starts in the village. Unfortunately, the Iron Age hillfort on the summit of Mam Tor has also suffered, and a considerable proportion of its original 16 acres has disappeared down the hillside.

To the west of Castleton is the unusual and spectacular gorge of Winnats Pass ★. Here are three of the show caves for which the town is renowned. Two of them — the Blue John and Treak Cliff — are old mines that worked some of the fourteen veins of Blue John in the area.

A Blue John table in the Ollerenshaw Collection, Castleton.

Eight of these were found in Blue John Cavern but the only viable source of the mineral today is at Treak Cliff. Blue John is found among the limestone, and beautiful, massive formations of stalactites and stalagmites are present in both caves. Several shops in the town sell jewellery made from the stone but the finest examples are to be seen in the Ollerenshaw Collection, one of the finest and largest collections of Blue John in the world.

Lead was also extracted here, but the eighteenth-century mine at Speedwell Cavern was a failure. The workings are of interest, though, and visitors are taken by boat along an illuminated ½-mile canal to the old mine face. The nearby Odin mine was a greater success — the Peak District's oldest recorded lead mine and one of the richest. It is not open to the public but the remains of a crushing circle can be seen just below the road underneath Mam Tor. It comprises a circular iron track upon which the lead ore would be heaped prior to crushing by a millstone, rolled around a pivot by a horse. Just to the south of the town lies Cave Dale, another dry gorge explored on **Walk 4**. Nearby Peak Cavern

is the fourth of the show caves with probably the most awe-inspiring approach of any cave in the country. The entrance is about 50 feet high and almost twice as wide — large enough to have contained several cottages. These were inhabited by ropemakers and a village tradition presented new Castleton brides with a locally made washing line. The former ropewalks can still be seen and only recently ceased operating.

Another local custom is the garlanding ceremony that takes place on Oak Apple Day, 29 May, supposedly in celebration of Charles II's escape by hiding in an oak tree. The ceremony centres on a Garland King and his lady who proceed on horseback visiting each of the six inns. It is certainly not a comfortable ride, for the King wears a bell-shaped frame bedecked with flowers that can weigh up to 60 pounds. This is topped by a posy called the 'queen', laid at the end of the procession on the war memorial. The main garland is hoisted up the church tower. This curious tradition is certainly older than the seventeenth century and its distant origins may derive from a pagan fertility festival. It is certainly worth a stroll around Castleton, with plenty to do on even the wettest days. There is a helpful Tourist Information centre for the undecided. The town is included on **Tours 3, 6, and 9**.

Chapel-en-le-Frith (110) (SK 0680) 4 miles SE of Hayfield

Driving through Chapel today, it is hard to imagine that the origin of its name denotes a chapel built in a forest clearing. The town site once stood within the boundaries of the Royal Forest of the High Peak, a large tract of land reserved for the royal hunt. With the demand for land and timber for smelting, the Forest gradually dwindled and, by the end of the seventeenth century, it had disappeared. The original chapel was built by the King's Foresters in 1225, but it was replaced by the present parish church in the fourteenth century. It may appear at first glance

The approach to Peak Cavern (left); and Odin Mine (below), near Castleton.

to be Georgian, however, for it was substantially rebuilt in the eighteenth century. The market cross and stocks in the cobbled market square are also medieval.

Chapel grew in administrative and judicial importance and, by the end of the last century, it was regarded as the 'Capital of the Peak'. It has declined somewhat since but is known internationally as the home of Ferodo brake linings. The company's location in the town is entirely fortuitous, and was begun by the inventive Herbert Frood, who noticed the way carters used old boots over their wooden brake blocks to slow down the carts. He emerged with his invention after experiments in his garden shed, which is still preserved by the company. Just over a mile to the north-west are the magnificent curving double stone viaducts of the old Midland Railway, towering over 100 feet above the road. They can be seen from **Tours 6** and **10**. Chapel-en-le-Frith is visited on **Tours 6**, **9**, and **10**.

Chatsworth (119) (SK 2670) 1½ miles SE of Baslow

Chatsworth has been home to the Cavendish family — later the Dukes of Devonshire — since the sixteenth century, and stands as one of the finest houses in Britain. Its exterior magnificence is matched by the treasure chest of art and antiques inside the house, and it easily earns its nickname of 'Palace of the Peak'. The present structure is not the first building on the site. That was completed by the formidable Bess of Hardwick in 1564 but little remains now apart from Queen Mary's Bower and the Hunting Tower in the woods behind the house. The existing house dates largely from the late seventeenth century, when the Fourth Earl (soon after elevated to Duke) decided to rebuild his inheritance. Apart from the addition of a north wing in the early nineteenth century, the exterior has changed little since the time of the first Duke.

The Devonshires' wealth was greatly augmented by revenues from their mining interests, including the vastly profitable copper mine at Ecton in the Manifold valley. Thus, they were able to amass an amazing private collection of priceless masterpieces of art, furniture, porcelain, and tapestries. They were also able to engage the services of the finest designers of the day, employing such as Capability Brown and Sir Joseph Paxton as 'gardeners'. James Paine built the two elegant bridges, the stable block, and the road that runs through the park. The grounds contain much of interest, including the famous Emperor Fountain, noted for being the highest gravity-fed fountain in the world. It is capable of sending up a 290-foot jet of water, the second highest in Europe. Behind the house water cascades over a series of terraced steps before disappearing underground. Also of note is the Azalea Dell, the formal gardens with their laburnum tunnel, and the farmyard and forestry exhibition established recently near the house.

The villages of Edensor and Pilsley were also part of the 'landscaping'. The old village of Edensor was completely removed by the Sixth Duke who considered that the buildings ob-

Chatsworth House, one of the finest houses in Britain.

structed the view from the House. Paxton planned the new village, built in 1838-42, to rehouse the inhabitants. He also designed some of the houses in Pilsley, which was extended to house some of the other villagers. In fine weather, Chatsworth can easily occupy a whole day with plenty to see in both House and grounds. It is included in **Tour 9**.

Chelmorton (119) (SK 1170) 4 miles SE of Buxton

There are several interesting features about this village. At its northern end lies a Bronze Age barrow near which rises the unforgettably named Illy Willy Water. Here is the oldest part of the village and, at 1200 feet, the medieval church is one of the highest in the country. Chelmorton is best known, though, for the striking pattern of dry stone walls that have 'fossilised' the narrow medieval strip fields. These stretch back at right-angles to the single main street and date from the coming of the first enclosure. In contrast are the neatly rectangular fields further away from the village laid out after an Enclosure Award in 1809.

Crich (119) (SK 3554) 4 miles west of Wirksworth

Crich is an attractive hill village, visited on **Tour 8**, with some interesting old buildings and

Two of the National Tramway Museum's exhibits at Crich.

Crich Stand, the memorial dedicated to the Sherwood Foresters who fell in the two World Wars.

Crich Stand, a memorial dedicated to the soldiers of the Sherwood Foresters who fell in the two World Wars. It stands at 950 feet and the views are said to extend from Lincoln Cathedral in the east as far as the Wrekin in the west.

Cromford (119) (SK 2956) 1¾ miles north of Wirksworth

Before the Industrial Revolution arrived in the late eighteenth century, Cromford was little more than a hamlet dependent on the usual combined Peak activities of agriculture and lead mining. This changed with the arrival of Richard Arkwright in 1771, however, and the establishment of the world's first water-powered cotton mill. He was attracted to Cromford by the water power available from the Bonsall Brook and Cromford Sough, and refused to be daunted by the lack of a workforce and poor communications. The consequent community development was one of the first of its kind in the country. Arkwright built three mills in the village, one of which — Masson Mill beside the A6 — still manufactures textiles. The others are situated along the Crich road and were acquired for preservation by the Arkwright Society in 1979. This is an interesting site with information boards and an audio-visual display explaining the history of the mills and warehouses.

The village itself was also part of Arkwright's scheme to provide for his workers. The neat gritstone terraces of North Street were built in 1777 and the Greyhound Hotel was completed the following year. His son built the school in 1832. The central pond was built to provide power for the mills. The nearby 14-foot diameter overshot waterwheel dates from the mid-nineteenth century and was restored to working order in 1975. The fine three-arched bridge over the Derwent to the north of the village is fifteenth century. On the east bank there is an eighteenth-century fishing pavilion and the ruins of a fifteenth-century bridge chapel. Willersley Castle to the west was one of Sir Richard Arkwright's residences, a solid Gothic edifice

monuments. Of particular note is a three-storey framework knitter's cottage dating from the eighteenth century and a multiple horse trough that served the needs of the packhorses with their cargoes of lead and stone. The village is noted, however, for the nearby National Tramway Museum, situated in a former limestone quarry owned by George Stephenson. This ceased working in 1957 and the Museum became established by 1959. It has since amassed a collection of over forty trams that range in age from 1874-1950. The visitor can ride along the mile-long section of track, and the sheds also contain a reconstructed Victorian street scene and an informative lead mining display.

Just above is the well-known landmark of

Young people learning to climb under Ranger supervision near Cromford.

Arkwright's first of three mills at Cromford.

built just before his death in 1792.

Near the bridge are the remaining buildings of Cromford Wharf, once a flourishing centre for both goods and passengers. It is the western terminus of the Cromford Canal, built by 1793 largely at Arkwright's instigation to aid the movement of raw materials and finished textiles to and from the mills. The Arkwright Society produces several leaflets on the town, available at Tourist Information Centres and at the mill site. **Tours 2, 8,** and **9** visit Cromford, and a stroll around the town and the mills is highly recommended.

Darley Dale (119) (SK 2762) 2¼ miles NW of Matlock

At first sight, there may not seem to be much of interest in this long, straggling settlement beside the A6. Somehow, the place does not live up to its rather romantic name, and most visitors pass through en route to Bakewell ★ or Matlock ★. This is a pity for the village has some noteworthy historical features and associations. Darley Dale is made up of the four settlements of Churchtown, Darley Hillside, Two Dales to the east of the Derwent near a springline, and Darley Bridge to the west. The parish church at Churchtown contains the fine fourteenth-century tomb of Sir John de Darley and a wall painting of a ship, possibly more than 400 years old. The oldest feature, however, is the Darley Yew in the graveyard, with a girth of 33 feet. The latest research puts its possible age at about 900 to 1000 years, which means it could pre-date the present church.

Darley Dale is probably best known as the home of Joseph Whitworth, inventor of, among other things, the Whitworth thread for nuts and bolts. He made his fortune and bought Stancliffe Hall on the eastern slopes of the valley just above the village. It was his intention to form a model village and to this end he built cottages for his estate workers, a hotel, a hospital and an institute.

There are also two museums of note in Darley Dale. The Derbyshire Museum and Arts Centre near the crossroads houses a varying programme of exhibitions in its theatre/exhibition hall and is also home to an eighty-seven-key Gavioli fairground organ, played at regular intervals. The Working Carriage Museum just to the south has one of the finest private collections of horse-drawn vehicles and equipment in the country. There are almost thirty carriages, which are regularly taken out on the road. Darley Dale is included on **Tours 2, 8,** and **9.**

Dovedale (119) (SK 1452) 2 miles W of Tissington

Dovedale has attracted many superlatives since its 'discovery' in the early nineteenth century when a new mood of romanticism swept the country. This is one of the most visited parts of the Peak, with the stepping stones below Thorpe Cloud possibly the best-known spot in the National Park. Thankfully, the dale is too narrow and steep for the continuation of a metalled road up the valley, and it remains largely the domain of the walker. The river is renowned for its trout and inspired the literary partnership of Izaak Walton and Charles Cotton, who were co-authors of *The Compleat Angler.* Cotton was

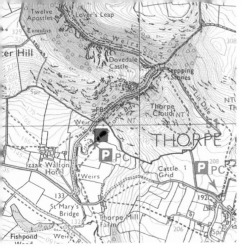

Reynard's Cave, Dovedale.

the squire at Beresford Hall and thought the Dove to be 'the princess of rivers'. He was referring more to the abundance of fish, but his writings encouraged a stream of visitors who came to admire the scenery of the dale.

The river rises on Axe Edge ★ and flows for 45 miles until it meets the Trent. In the Peak it is flanked by some remarkable and unexpectedly spectacular limestone scenery, and the walker is often enticed around the next bend out of curiosity. Its course through the Peak can be divided into several sections. In its upper reaches, it flows through a fairly broad valley with a series of pronounced reef limestone 'peaks' on the east, in contrast to the subdued shale and gritstone country on the west. Below Hartington ★ , the river valley becomes more like a gorge as it cuts through the limestone. Somewhat confusingly, it becomes known in

Thorpe Cloud, easily climbed, gives excellent views from its summit.

turn as Beresford Dale and Wolfscote Dale. At Milldale it is crossed by the charming old pack-horse bridge now known as Viator's Bridge, after which is the section most people recognise as Dovedale — the stretch of river some 3 to 4 miles long which contains most of the well-known features such as Dove Holes, Pickering Tor, Ilam Rock, Reynard's Cave, Tissington Spires and, of course, the stepping stones.

Dovedale is also renowned for its relict ash woodland and for this reason has been declared a Site of Special Scientific Interest (SSSI). Much of this section of the Dale belongs to the National Trust as part of their South Peak Estate. The dale's southern entrance is guarded by Bunster Hill and Thorpe Cloud — the latter an easily climbed cone–shaped peak rising to 942 feet and affording excellent views from its summit. Dovedale may seem to be enduringly beautiful but, in reality, it is rather more fragile and has suffered considerably in recent years from visitor pressure. The Park has responded by constructing well-made paths alongside large sections of the river so that most visitors today have access to the wonderful scenery of the dale. A stroll from the car park just below Thorpe Cloud would at least give a taste of Dovedale and is highly recommended. **Tour 1** passes through Thorpe and Hartington, and **Tour 2** passes through Milldale and Hartington. There are wonderful views of the peaks in the upper dale from **Tours 4, 7,** and **9.** Walkers can explore the dale further on **Walks 2** and **9.**

Ecton (119) (SK 0958) ³/₄ mile east of Warslow
Above Ecton, the Manifold flows along a broad and shallow valley across the shales. The 1212-foot dome of Ecton Hill, however, marks its arrival on to the limestone into which it has cut a deep gorge. Ecton is a tiny hamlet and it is difficult to imagine now that this was once the site of considerable industrial activity centring around one of the largest copper mines in Europe of its time. Copper was discovered and first worked here in the middle of the seventeenth century but production later increased markedly with the introduction of gunpowder — Ecton claims to be among the first mines to use the material. Unlike most other mines in the Peak, Ecton was not troubled by flooding and was an exceptionally productive and profitable undertaking for the Dukes of Devonshire, who owned the mineral rights.

Production reached a peak in 1786 when about 4000 tons of ore were extracted, and between 1760 and 1817 the mine produced an estimated profit of £335,000. Even more staggering is the £1,300,000 profit earned during the eighteenth century as a whole. It is hardly surprising then that Chatsworth ★ acquired such palatial dimensions and became so richly endowed with priceless furniture and works of art. It is also generally held that the Fifth Duke paid for the construction of The Crescent at Buxton ★ — at a cost of £38,000 — out of profits from the mine. Mining ceased in the late nineteenth century, and all that remains now are some abandoned buildings and workings, and the waste tips scarring the side of Ecton Hill. Ecton is included on **Tour 2.**

Kinder Downfall (top); its scale can be judged by looking at the walkers on the right of the picture; and the peat hags and groughs of Kinder Scout (above) show the isolation of Edale.

Edale (110) (SK 1285) 2 miles NW of Castleton
Until the coming of the Sheffield-Manchester railway in 1894, the Edale valley was largely undiscovered. It is an isolated spot, fairly appreciated from **Tour 10,** that is tightly enclosed between the Kinder Scout ★ plateau to the north and the Mam Tor ★ -Lose Hill ridge to the south. Sunshine is a precious commodity here and most of the old houses and farms lie on the southern slopes of Kinder Scout. Edale itself is a loose collection of scattered hamlets or 'booths' that grew around the original shelters or 'bothies' used by shepherds when tending their flocks on the hillside. The main village is part of Grindsbrook Booth, one of a series stretching west-east from Upper, Barber, Ollerbrook to Nether Booth.

Today, Edale fairly bustles with visitors, many of them intent on outdoor activities. In winter, it is popular with skiers, and it is one of the most popular walking centres in the Peak, lying as it does so close to the Kinder plateau and at the southern end of the 250-mile long Pennine Way. This takes two routes from the village — one leading north up Grindsbrook and the other heading west towards Jacob's Ladder. They rejoin at Kinder Downfall on the western edge of Kinder Scout plateau then cross the peat bogs towards Bleaklow. The plateau forms the highest land in the National Park at 2088 feet, and should not be explored unless properly equipped for rough terrain and the possibility of bad weather. Weather information is available from the National Park Information Centre, which also houses an interesting exhibition on local history. Edale, in fact, was the site of the first mountain rescue post, beginning unofficially with the efforts of one of the landlords of the

Nag's Head pub and some of his customers. The network expanded and grew into the Peak District Mountain Rescue Organisation. The inn itself dates from 1577 and possibly arose from the custom of the packhorse teams carrying salt across the Peak from Cheshire. An old packhorse bridge still spans the Grinds Brook.

Eyam (119) (SK 2176) 1¼ miles NW of Stoney Middleton

Eyam (pronounced 'Eem') is a busy mining and quarrying village with a long history, but will forever be remembered for the courage displayed in two fateful years in the seventeenth century when it was almost overcome by a visitation of the dreaded bubonic plague. From 1665-66, two thirds of the village — 259 people — fell victim to the disease. It is thought to have arrived in a box of cloth sent from London and spread rapidly through the population. The rector, William Mompesson, managed to persuade the villagers to undertake a self-imposed quarantine to contain the disease and arranged for supplies of food to be left at collection points. One such place is Mompesson's Well, lying just to the north of the village. In an attempt to reduce the risk of infection, Mompesson closed the church and held his services in the open air at Cucklet Delf, a natural limestone cavern just to the south. A remembrance service is held here every August. Many of the dead were buried in rough, unmarked graves. Some memorials can be seen, however, such as the Riley Graves to the east of the village. The isolated walled enclosure contains the remains of seven members of the Hancock family, all of whom died within the space of eight days.

From the Graves the view to the south is dominated by the ugly scars of a fluorspar mine and you are quickly transported — perhaps with relief — once again back to the twentieth century. Fluorspar is now the most commonly extracted mineral but lead was once very important in the Eyam area. It is thought to have been worked in Roman times and reached peak production in the early eighteenth century with the discovery of new deposits. Mounting costs and competition caused a decline in lead production but other industries sprang up. First, cotton in the mid-eighteenth century, then silk, and then shoes were manufactured in the village. The shoes were widely exported, and the last factory continued production until 1979. The churchyard contains much of interest including an eighth-century Saxon cross, outstanding for its carving and completeness. Nearby is Catherine Mompesson's grave and an unusual sundial of 1775 that gives the time in different parts of the world. Inside, there is a Saxon font, wall paintings dating from about 1600, and Mompesson's chair, dated 1665.

The Riley Graves (below), a memorial to seven members of one family who fell victim to the plague at Eyam. Right: The churchyard contains an eighth-century Saxon cross.

There are many attractive buildings in the village displaying a variety of architectural styles. Near the church are Plague Cottages, where the plague first arrived in the village. Behind the ball-topped gateway in the main street lies Eyam Hall, rebuilt in 1676 from the materials of Bradshaw Hall. The ruins of the latter building stand near the car park. The roasting spit nearby stands on a green field that used to be the village pond, and the interesting double horse trough accommodated both horses and dogs. The old market hall and stocks have been renovated and still stand at the western end of the village. The Square in the centre of Eyam contains several interesting features including an iron ring set in a stone used for bull and bear baiting.

Allow plenty of time for a stroll around Eyam. You could follow the village trail mapped out on the display board at the door of the market hall or purchase one of the informative guide books from the church. Eyam is included on **Tours 6** and **10**.

Fairholmes (110) (SK 1789) 3½ miles N of Hope The car park is sited at the northern end of Ladybower Reservoir just below Derwent Dam. It has been pleasantly laid out and the careful landscaping, using deciduous trees and grassy banks, won a conservation award. Various birds and animals are attracted to the site and it is possible to see a good variety of wildlife just by sitting quietly in your car. You could well be rewarded by seeing squirrels and jays at close quarters.

Fairholmes is a good base from which to explore the Upper Derwent, and it lies at the centre of a network of footpaths. As part of a traffic management scheme, cars are not allowed further north on Sundays and Bank Holidays from Easter to the end of November, disabled drivers excepted. The road east to Mill Brook is closed to the public all year round. Provisions have been made, though, for exploration further into the valley, and visitors can either walk, hire a bicycle, or catch the regular

Top: the Derwent Dam holds back the waters of the Ladybower Reservoir (centre). Bottom: the carefully landscaped car park below the Derwent Dam won a conservation award.

minibus service that runs on the days when the road north is forbidden to public traffic.

Immediately upstream of the car park lies Derwent Dam, holding back a reservoir of some 176 acres with a capacity of over 2000 million gallons of water. This Gothic gritstone structure was completed in 1916 and may not be to everyone's taste, but most would agree that the sight and sound of water spilling over the dam face is impressive. Nearby is Tip's Memorial, which commemorates the touching story of a faithful sheepdog who stayed by her dead master for fifteen weeks until he was found on the surrounding high moors in the winter of 1954. The Upper Derwent was selected as a training ground for the famous dambusting 617 squadron in 1943 due to its similarity to the Ruhr Valley. There is an interesting display on this and other aspects of the history of the valley inside the Information Centre. The paths near the car park are clearly waymarked and a stroll around Fairholmes is recommended. It is included on **Tours 5** and **10** and also forms the start point of **Walk 5**.

Flagg (119) (SK 1468) 1½ miles NW of Monyash
Situated high up on dry, open moorland, Flagg owes it existence to lead mining, and the presence of a small mere — much like Monyash ★ just to the south-east. Its buildings are stretched out along the main street and, at the eastern end, is a fine Elizabethan Hall. The land round about is pitted with former lead workings, attesting to the earlier importance of the industry. Nowadays, of course, it is more concerned with farming and assumes significant local importance every Easter Tuesday when it becomes the site of the High Peak Hunt point-to-point races. These are held near the A515 close to the unusually named Bull I' Thorn Inn — thought to date from the fifteenth century — and are reputed to be the highest meeting of its kind in the country.

The graceful packhorse bridge at Three Shires Head.

Flash (119) (SK 0267) 4½ miles SW of Buxton
In winter, few would dispute the village claim of being the highest in England. Naturally, the village inn and parish church also claim the distinction. Lying at over 1500 feet on Axe Edge ★ , it occupies a rather exposed, windswept location on the western gritstone moorland.

Tradition has it that some of the villagers spent the long, dark winter evenings counterfeiting money which became known as 'flash' from its place of manufacture. Just over a mile to the north-west lies Three Shires Head, a beautiful spot containing a graceful packhorse bridge and small waterfalls, which was reputedly used by the counterfeiters to escape into Cheshire when the trail became too hot! The village is included on **Tour 7**.

Foolow (119) (SK 1976) 1½ miles W of Eyam
Foolow clusters around its green and spring-fed mere — both rare features in the Peak. The

The fourteenth-century cross by the village green and mere at Foolow.

cross is fourteenth century and may once have marked the boundary of the Royal Forest of the Peak. It was placed in its present position in 1868 next to a bull-baiting stone similar to that in the centre of Eyam ★. It must be fairly old because bull baiting was made illegal in 1835. Foolow once relied on lead mining and farming, but today it is occupied mainly by commuters who have converted and restored the old buildings into attractive residences. Many of the buildings date from the seventeenth and eighteenth centuries, including the manor house and the Spread Eagle Inn. The village can be seen from **Tour 10**.

Glossop (110) (SK 0394)

There are really two parts to the town, and most people miss the original gritstone village of Old Glossop to the east of the main town centre. This is a pity, for it contains the parish church, the old market square, and some lovely seventeenth-century cottages. The main part of Glossop to the west is in fact a 'new' town planned by the Twelfth Duke of Norfolk in the early nineteenth century in response to the growth of the local cotton industry. Howard Town, as it was called, was well laid out with a fine square and some notable buildings including the Town Hall of 1838 and the Market Hall, 1845. The mills prospered and the town's population swelled to 26,000. Hurst Reservoir was constructed on the moorland to the east in 1837 to supply the cotton mills, and a branch line brought trains into the town from the Sheffield-Manchester railway in Longdendale. Glossop's fortune declined with the slump of the cotton trade early

this century but it has retained its civic dignity. The Heritage Centre in the square has a fascinating display of artefacts from the town's past and a lot of interesting historical information.

Glossop seems strangely out of place in Derbyshire because, in appearance and character, it has far more in common with the industrial cotton towns of Lancashire. This presumably was one of the reasons for its exclusion from the National Park, which surrounds the town in a neat semi-circle. In fact, the moorland is so close that it is possible in ten minutes to drive east from the grand buildings in Norfolk Square along the A57 and ascend to 1600 feet where the Pennine Way crosses the road. The sudden contrast from civilisation to wilderness is startling — not to mention the drop in temperature! The A57 is the infamous Snake Road, frequently closed in winter. It derived its name ultimately from the snake crest of the Dukes of Devonshire, as seen on the sign of the Snake Inn at the bottom of Lady Clough. Not far from the road on Coldharbour moor are some exposed kerbstones and paving slabs that are now believed to be a medieval imposition on an original Roman road. This would have connected the fort at Ardotalia, to the north-west of present-day Glossop, with that at Navio, near Brough. Doctor's Gate, as it is known, is named after Dr John Talbot, a vicar of Glossop from 1494-1550 who presumably used the old route with fair regularity to cross the moor.

Glossop has few airs and graces, and its solid, unpretentious buildings present a workaday countenance. Both the new and the old towns are worth a stroll, which may be added on to **Tours 5** and **10**.

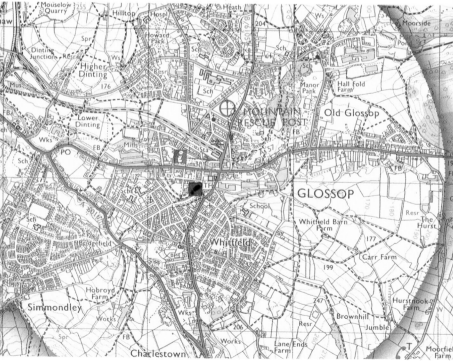

GRINDLEFORD

Grindleford (119) (SK 2478) 2½ miles NE of Eyam

Grindleford lies at the point where the Eyam, Hathersage, and Fox House Inn roads meet to cross the Derwent. It is also served by a railway, part of the Hope Valley line that opened in 1894. The station is located to the north, actually in Upper Padley, and lies at the western end of Totley Tunnel. This considerable feat of engineering took almost six years to construct and, at a length of 3 miles and 950 yards, it is second only to that under the Severn. The station lies close to the Burbage Brook, which descends steeply amid mossy boulders and beautiful woodland. Access to the wood and the riverside path is from the road just above the station.

Just ¼ mile to the west of the station lies Padley Chapel, formerly the gatehouse to Padley Hall which now lies in ruins to the rear. This was once the home of the devout Catholic Fitzherbert family, and every year in July becomes a site of pilgrimage. This marks an event in less tolerant times of two Catholic priests found hiding here in 1588 and who were put to death shortly after in a gruesome manner. The gatehouse was later used as a barn but, in 1933, it was bought up by the Nottingham Catholic

Below: *Padley Chapel, formerly the gatehouse to Padley Hall.*
Bottom: *The attractive Padley Gorge.*

More than a million tons of gritstone were taken from nearby Grindleford for use in the construction of the Howden (above) *and Derwent Dams.*

Diocese and converted into a chapel. The hillside high above the chapel was the site of Bole Hill Quarry which, early this century, produced some one-and-a-quarter million tons of gritstone for the construction of the Derwent and Howden dams.

To the north-east of Grindleford is the Longshaw Estate, acquired by the National Trust in 1927 from the Duke of Rutland and scene each September of the Longshaw Sheepdog Trial. Grindleford is incorporated on **Tours 6** and **10**.

Haddon Hall (119) (SK 2366) 1¾ miles SE of Bakewell

Compared to Chatsworth's massive proportions, Haddon is positively 'homely'. Unlike Chatsworth, however, it was built up over several centuries and has been so beautifully restored that it is regarded as one of the finest medieval manor houses in the country. It has been owned by only a handful of families and owes its exceptional state of preservation to its abandonment by the Manners — later the Dukes of Rutland — in 1640 in favour of their other residence at Belvoir Castle. Thus, it escaped any modifications or additions from Georgian and Victorian owners and lay largely neglected until early this century when the Ninth Duke of Rutland began a thorough restoration.

The first building here was owned by the Norman William Peveril, who also built the castle at Castleton ★. Some Norman work still remains in the chapel. The superb banqueting hall with its oak panelling and open fireplace has remained largely unaltered since it was built in about 1350. History seems to emanate from every corner — even the table is 400 years old. The whole house contains much sixteenth-century work, and it seems that every room is a historical gem. The Hall has been immortalised in literature by Sir Walter Scott from its association with the elopement of Dorothy Vernon and John Manners in 1563. She is supposed to have fled down the steps leading from the long gallery to meet her lover on the packhorse bridge over the Wye, but the story becomes less believable because both these features were built by the couple some twenty-six years after their marriage!

Visitors have to use the car park across the A6 from the Hall and this can be reached from **Tour 8**.

Hartington (119) (SK 1360) 3½ miles NE of Warslow

The beautiful rolling countryside of the Dove Valley near Hartington.

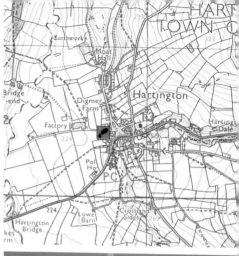

Hartington is an attractive limestone village in the upper Dove Valley, with a mere and large market place at its centre. In fact, it was granted the first recorded market charter in the Peak in 1203. Although it caters well for the tourist with its cafés and craft shops, the village has retained its character. The town hall dates from 1836 and the church contains some thirteenth- to fourteenth-century work with three seventeenth-century bells in the tower.

The cheese shop in the market place sells products made in the Hartington Stilton Cheese Factory just to the west. The cheese is exported around the world, and Hartington is the last reminder of a once thriving Derbyshire cheese-making tradition. The splendid youth hostel up the hill on the eastern side of the village was once Hartington Hall, a typical Peakland manor house built in 1611 but enlarged in the nineteenth century. The village had close associations with Charles Cotton, of *Compleat Angler* fame, who lived at Beresford Hall in Beresford Dale. The Charles Cotton Hotel contains some of his drawings and poetry. A mile to the south of the village lies the fishing house he built in 1674.

About 1¼ miles to the east of Hartington is a

Above: *The attractive limestone village of Hartington. It is hard to believe that, until early this century, Haddon Hall (below) lay largely neglected.*

signal box by the former Ashbourne-Buxton line. This section of the track closed in 1967 and now forms part of the Tissington Trail. The building has been converted into an interesting information centre and contains the lever frames and photographs of the old railway. The strange earthworks at Pilsbury Castle 2½ miles to the north are the best-preserved example of a Norman motte and bailey castle in the Peak. Little is known about it, however, and it may occupy the site of an Iron Age fort.

Hartington is included in **Tours 1** and **2** and it is recommended that the visitor finds time to stroll around the village.

Hathersage (110) (SK 2381) 2 miles SW of Bamford

Hathersage is the main settlement of the middle Derwent valley with good rail and road communications. It is an attractive gritstone village that is well served with shopping and accommodation facilities but which has, nevertheless, successfully maintained its Peakland character. The area around Hathersage has long been associated with the manufacture of millstones and grindstones, and it is thought that querns were being made here in the late Iron Age. The millstone makers were superb craftsmen and their products were used not only to grind corn but also for crushing lead ore (as seen at the Odin Mine near Castleton ★), making paint, pulping wood, and crushing rape. Grindstones were in great demand in the Sheffield mills until the introduction of artificial abrasives at the end of the last century.

The village further prospered with the establishment of a needle industry in the early nineteenth century; five mills formed the centre of a needle, button, and wire-drawing industry. The smoke produced turned Hathersage into a dirty mill town until the industry's demise at the turn of this century. Most of the imposing mill buildings remain, however, now converted to other uses.

Hathersage has two notable historical associations. The first is with the legend of Robin Hood, who is said to have been born only 8 miles away at Loxley. In the churchyard is a 10-foot long grave from which a 30-inch thigh bone was exhumed in 1784, unfortunately since stolen. Tradition has it that this was part of the skeleton of Little John, apparently a native of Hathersage who, from this evidence, would have been around 7 feet tall. The second lies with the visit of Charlotte Brontë in 1845, when she stayed with her friends the Nusseys at the vicarage. Hathersage is the village of 'Morton' in *Jane Eyre*, and the heroine's surname was probably inspired by the ancient Eyre family who had been lords of the manor since Norman times. Robert Eyre is said to have built seven houses for his seven sons within sight of one another, and himself, around Hathersage. One of these — the sixteenth-century North Lees Hall — is thought to be 'Thornfield' in the novel.

Hathersage contains a considerable number of other interesting features and many of these are pointed out in the village trail produced by the local historical society, obtainable from the church and other places. It would be a useful addition to the recommended stroll. The village is visited on **Tours 3**, **6**, **9**, and **10**.

Hayfield (110) (SK 0386) 3¾ miles S of Glossop

Hayfield lies compactly along the Sett Valley just outside the western edge of the National Park. It is one of the walkers' 'gateways' to the Peak, with paths leading eastwards from the village on to the Kinder Scout ★ plateau. Some of these paths were used in centuries past by packhorse teams and, long before the Industrial Revolution came to the town, Hayfield held some importance as the meeting place of several of these old trading routes. The town changed, though, in the eighteenth century with the introduction of woollen weaving stimulated by increased demand from the burgeoning populations of Manchester and Stockport. At first it was a cottage industry carried out in the tall attics of three-storeyed buildings that can still be seen around the town centre. Later, the cloth was woven in mills powered by the River Sett. Other industries were established, encouraged initially by the availability of water power — cotton, cloth printing, and paper manufacturing. Some of these converted to steam but most fell victim to competition, and now only one mill remains operational at Little Hayfield.

Despite its industrial legacy — presumably one reason for its exclusion from the National Park — Hayfield is an attractive town containing many eighteenth-century stone cottages dating

The plaque (top) *commemorating the 'mass trespass' on to Kinder Scout from Hayfield* (above).

from the heyday of the cloth industry. The Packhorse Inn and the George Hotel date from the sixteenth century, and the latter hostelry claims proudly to be the place where George Hutchinson first heard the song that he later helped to popularise nationally as *Come Lads and Lasses*. Despite being outside the Park boundary, Hayfield had a crucial role to play in the formation of not only the Peak District but also every other National Park in the country. It was from Bowden Bridge quarry on the eastern edge of the town in 1932 that Benny Rothman led several hundred people on a mass trespass on to Kinder Scout as part of the struggle for public access to open land. A distinctive plaque now commemorates the start point of the route they took on to the moorland.

Walkers have continued to flock into the town ever since, it seems, intent not only on exploring the high, wild land to the east but also to ramble along the much gentler gradients of the Sett Valley Trail. This 2-mile track follows the former railway line from Hayfield to New Mills, closed

in 1970. Hayfield is included on **Tour 10** and the visitor is recommended to take time to stroll around the town. An inexpensive and informative guide and town trail is on sale in the shops.

High Peak Junction (119) (SK 3155) 1¼ miles SE of Cromford
When Richard Arkwright came to Cromford ★ in the eighteenth century, he quickly foresaw difficulties in transporting raw materials and finished goods from his mills. To this end, he was the driving force behind the construction of the 14-mile Cromford Canal, completed in 1794 to provide a link with the large industrial towns of Manchester, Liverpool, and Nottingham. At High Peak Junction, it meets the southern terminus of the 33-mile long Cromford and High Peak Railway, built to improve further communications into and out of this part of the Derwent Valley. It linked the Cromford Canal to the Peak Forest Canal at Whaley Bridge and was one of the earliest lines in the country when it opened in 1830. Its design seems to have been influenced by canal construction, and there are long, level sections between steep inclines (in place of locks) — even the stations are called wharfs. Originally horses were used on the level sections, and stationary steam engines pulled the wagons up the inclines. The last section of line stayed open until 1967 after which the track was adapted into the 17-mile High Peak Trail.

Among the interesting collection of buildings at High Peak Junction is the Wharf Shed, where goods were transferred between the canal and the railway. The former workshop has been converted into a visitor centre with a forge, an exhibition, and a video programme about the railway. Nearby is an old wagon caught in the catchpit at the bottom of Sheep Pasture Incline, a 1320-yard section of line varying in gradient between 1 in 8 and 1 in 9. About ¼ mile further south along the canal is Leawood Pump House with its imposing 95-foot high chimney. This was built in 1849 to solve the problem of water supply for the canal and houses a Cornish-type beam engine capable of pumping 20-30 tons of water a minute from the Derwent. It has been restored to working condition by the Cromford Canal Society and is steamed periodically. Just a little way further on is the Wigwell aqueduct, 200 yards long and 30 feet high. Much of the original structure had to be rebuilt soon after its

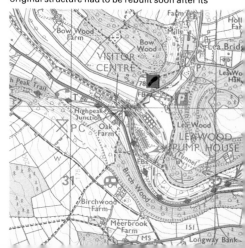

The Leawood Pump House, High Peak Junction.

the most extensive parishes in England including Buxton ★, Padley, Tideswell ★, and Chapel-en-le-Frith ★. It remained one of the largest until the last century. Today, the village is perhaps best known from its proximity to the the nearby cement works with its prominent chimney. Although it is such an eyesore, it was in existence long before the creation of the National Park and provides many valuable local jobs.

There are only a few reminders of Hope's early importance; among these is a lovely armless Saxon cross and a Norman font. Most of the church dates from 1200-1400, including the broach spire — unusual in the Peak. There are several notable features inside and, if the church is visited, the two thirteenth-century slabs, the sixteenth-century Breeches Bible, and seventeenth-century pulpit should not be missed.

In the village itself are a few buildings of note. The Old Hall Hotel was originally a manor house built in the early seventeenth century and Daggers House opposite was built in the next century as an inn. Hope dresses three wells in June and is scene on August Bank Holiday of the Hope Show and its well-known sheepdog trials. It is incorporated in **Tours 3**, **6**, **9**, and **10**.

construction owing to instability in the stonework.

Although the features of the site are of an industrial nature, the countryside is peaceful and makes a pleasant walk. The stroll is highly recommended and could be additional to **Tour 8**.

Hope (110) (SK 1783) 1½ miles E of Castleton
Hope lies at the confluence of the Peakshole Water and the River Noe, where the Vale of Edale joins the Hope Valley. It may seem overshadowed now by neighbouring Castleton ★ but, in Saxon times, it lay at the centre of one of

A fine example of well dressing — this is one of three found in the village of Hope.

Ilam (119) (SK 1350) 1½ miles W of Thorpe
Ilam was greatly altered by the Victorians. It was rebuilt by the shipping magnate, John Watts Russell, in the 1820s in an attempt to create a 'model' village. The church was restored by Gilbert Scott in 1855. A little of the original village still survives in the church, however, with the Saxon shrine of St Bertelin (or Bertram) and two crosses from the same period. The youth hostel is all that remains of Ilam Hall, a Tudor Gothic-style hall built for Russell between 1821-26 and probably modelled on Alton Towers. It was largely demolished in 1934 and handed over to the National Trust, who have since established a series of delightful riverside paths and a 1-mile nature trail in the grounds. The village, of course, has a wonderful location at the confluence of those two outstanding Peakland rivers — the Dove and the Manifold. In fact, the Manifold reappears at the 'Boil Hole' in the grounds of Ilam Hall after disappearing into its bed some 4 miles upstream at Wetton Mill. The village can be seen on **Tour 1**.

Nearby to the village of Hope is the vast bulk of the cement works.

The Ilam monument.

Kinder Scout (110) (SK 0988) 2½ miles NW of Edale

It may seem surprising to some that the 5 square miles of peat and heather north of Edale ★ lying at the very edge of the Pennines is one of the most popular and well-known parts of the Peak. It is renowned as the highest point in the Park and as the start — or end — of the 250-mile Pennine Way. This long-distance path offers two alternative routes from Edale, ascending to the plateau either by Grinds Brook or Jacob's Ladder. From the top, it proceeds north past the top of Kinder Downfall and on towards Bleaklow ★ . It is the most visited of the high northern

Kinder Scout — the start of the 250-mile long Pennine Way.

moors, and the boots of countless walkers have carved the infamous 'Pennine Motorway' into the soggy peat. The Park authorities have given high priority to the problem and have experimented with sections of well-drained paving surfaces.

The summit is a broad, featureless plateau — a 'disconsolate, bog quaking, ink oozing moor' according to John Derry in his classic guide *Across the Derbyshire Moors*. John Hillaby thought that the miles of sticky peat resemble manure and, although they seem lifeless, there is more wildlife than there seems to be at first sight, including grouse and the occasional mountain hare. The plateau reaches 2088 feet somewhere north-west of Crowden Tower but the actual summit is indiscernible among the mounds of peat Groups of weirdly shaped tors break the skyline, their names often realistically reflecting their outlines — the Boxing Glove Stones, the Pagoda, the Woolpacks.

On the western edge of the plateau, the Kinder River plunges 100 feet over the gritstone in a deluge that can be spectacular after wet weather. In a strong westerly wind the water is blown back towards the plateau but the waterfall is at its most stunning during the harsh months of winter when the cascade can become frozen into a curtain of icicles. At the bottom of the fall is Mermaid's Pool and local legend has it that the resident grants immortality to those who make such a request on Easter morning. There are various theories regarding the origin of the plateau's unusual name. It may have come from the Old English *Kyndwr Scut*, meaning 'water over the edge' and possibly refers to the waterfall. Alternatively, 'Kinder' may derive from an ancient British word later added to *skuti*, a Norse word meaning a high, overhanging rock.

Kinder has a special significance for walkers and all who hold dearly the right to roam the countryside, for the plateau was the scene of the famous access battles of the 1930s. At that time

both Kinder and Bleaklow were jealously guarded grouse moors, and 15 square miles of Kinder were completely lacking in public paths. These confrontations with the owners and their gamekeepers culminated in the Trespass of 1932 and ultimately, it could be said, in the creation of the National Parks themselves. There are good views of the plateau from **Walk 4** and **5**, and **Tour 10** passes through Edale ★ .

Lathkill and Bradford Dale (119) (SK 1866)
There is much to commend these two lovely valleys, including the absence of traffic and the necessity of exploration on foot. In wet weather, the Lathkill issues impressively from a cave not far from the 'confluence' with Cales Dale. In

drier conditions, it emerges some way further down the valley. It is an exceptional river — the only one in the Peak District and one of very few in the country which has its entire catchment area and flows its whole length on limestone. It is one of the purest rivers in the country as indicated by the continuing deposition of calcium carbonate — or tufa — in the mill pool of the ruined corn mill in the upper part of the valley. It has also long been appreciated for its fish and, according to Charles Cotton, co-author of *The Compleat Angler*, '...bred the reddest and the best Trouts in England.'

The dale was designated a National Nature Reserve by the Nature Conservancy Council in 1972, largely on account of its rich flora and fauna. Included among these are some national rarities like mezereon and Jacob's ladder. Others occur high up on the crags where the steep slopes discouraged human activity. The ash woods along the southern bank of the river represent some of the finest 'climax' ash wood in Britain, but the trees on the north bank were planted largely after the cessation of mining activities in the nineteenth century. Today the dale seems peaceful enough but, at times in the past, it was a relative hive of activity connected with the extraction of various minerals. Black marble, ochre, and even gold — there was a minor 'goldrush' in 1854-56 for what turned out to be iron pyrites (fool's gold) — have been dug out of the dale. Lead, though, was the most important and it is possible it was mined as early as the eleventh century.

Until the eighteenth century, mining occurred on a small scale but two main mines eventually emerged and instigated engineering projects to work the deeper deposits and solve the flooding problems. The river was canalised between artificial banks on a puddled clay bed and a leat was constructed to supply water to a water-

Left: *A useful notice at the entrance to Lathkill Dale, shows the extent of the National Nature Reserve.*
Below: *It is well worth the trip in to the dale itself.*

A typical Dales view, with dry stone walls as far as the eye can see. This is near Litton.

wheel at each mine. The wheel at Lathkill mine was enormous — 52 feet in diameter and one of the largest in the country. A Cornish beam engine was installed at Mandale Mine in the 1840s but both enterprises remained unprofitable and closed in the mid-nineteenth century. There are still a few remains of the mine buildings beside the river.

Bradford Dale meets the Lathkill at Alport ★, a charming village with its old cottages and ancient bridge. Upstream below Youlgreave ★, the river flows unexpectedly into six clear ponds which, with the packhorse and clapper bridges, make this a particularly delightful stretch of the dale. Lomberdale Hall near the head of the dale was home to Thomas Bateman, archaeologist extraordinary, who lies buried in the chapel he had built at Middleton.

Both dales are explored on **Walk 1**. There are no roads along the valleys but **Tour 1** visits Youlgreave.

Litton (119) (SK 1675) 1 mile SW of Tideswell
Litton occupies a lofty position almost 1000 feet up on the limestone plateau above the Wye. It has a pleasantly open arrangement along the main street with a triangular green at its western end and grass verges down both sides. Behind these are rows of attractive buildings, many dating from the seventeenth and eighteenth centuries. About ½ mile to the east at the head of Cressbrook Dale is the prominent outcrop of limestone known as Peter's Stone. The dale is often dry at this point — the brook generally makes its appearance just a little further down. This lovely dale is accessible to the public and the footpaths offer very pleasant walking along the valley bottom.

Cressbrook Mill at the lower end of the dale lies in a section of the Wye known delightfully as Water cum Jolly Dale. This former textile mill was built in 1815 to replace an earlier mill established by Arkwright in 1779. The handsome and well-proportioned main building is slowly being restored where it is occupied but, unfortunately,

remains largely empty and neglected. The row of cottages behind was once occupied by the apprentices, who were apparently rather better treated here than in neighbouring Litton Mill just to the west. According to Robert Blincoe, an apprentice at the mill from 1803-14, the masters were cruel and the conditions harsh. His memoirs may have been deliberately overly melodramatic but Litton Mill retained its reputation for exploiting child labour.

The village is included in **Tour 1**.

Longdendale (110) (SK 0799 — Crowden in middle of valley)
Longdendale is the name given to the valley of the River Etherow where it flows westwards off the northern moors above Glossop. The Normans established it as the northern boundary of the Royal Forest of the Peak and, in the Domesday Book, recorded it as 'waste'. There are many who would consider that things have changed little for the Etherow is definitely not one of the more remote and unspoilt dales. Crammed into this somewhat crowded valley are five reservoirs, a railway, power lines, and a main road. The reservoirs supply around twenty-four million gallons of water a day for Manchester and were constructed between 1848 and 1875. Their financial cost was over three million pounds but there was a further price to pay in the break up of the once thriving communities at Crowden and Woodhead, ordered in the interests of water purity.

The railway is now closed but was once part of the Great Central Manchester-Sheffield line and entailed construction of the Woodhead Tunnel. In fact, there have been three in all, the first completed in 1845 and the last in 1953. The tunnel gained some notoriety for the number of accidents and deaths that occurred during its construction in the nineteenth century with numerous injuries and over thirty fatalities. Humankind has greatly scarred the landscape here but the surrounding wild moors seem to be able to absorb a lot of the ugliness, and the area remains popular with walkers. Longdendale is incorporated on **Tour 5**.

One of the five reservoirs, supplying Manchester with millions of gallons of water per day, in the valley of the River Etherow, known as Longdendale.

Longnor (119) (SK 0864) 3¾ miles NW of Hartington

The village stands on a ridge between the Dove and the Manifold just inside the northern boundary of Staffordshire. The lovely cobbled market square reflects Longnor's former importance as a trading centre, and at the top end is the market hall, erected in 1873. Earlier, the village had benefited from the construction of several turnpike roads and lay at an important crossroads. The stage coaches passed through and the inns prospered. The railway never arrived in Longnor, however, and with the setting in of an agricultural depression later in the nineteenth century, the village began to fade and its population declined. Recently, though, Longnor has revived somewhat. It was declared a Conservation Area in 1977 and has undergone restoration by the National Park. In 1981 it became part of the Peak's Integrated Rural Development experiment in which the villagers themselves proposed ideas for conservation and community projects. The Park authority co-ordinated and integrated the grants available for such schemes with the resulting establishment of craft workshops and a small industrial estate.

A stroll around this attractive village is recommended and could be appended to **Tours 4, 7,** and **9.** There are interesting narrow 'jitties' between the solid, stone cottages. Also worth a look is the church, restored in the Classic Georgian style in 1780 and which contains a memorial to William Bellinge — said to have lived for

The solid, stone cottages of Longnor.

112 years. Around Longnor is some of the most outstanding scenery in the Peak. The upper Dove to the north-west is lined on one side with spectacular conical hills of reef limestone. High Wheeldon (1383 feet) to the north-east was given to the National Trust in memory of the Derbyshire and Staffordshire men killed in the last war.

Lyme Hall (109) (SJ 9682) 7 miles NW of Buxton

Lyme Hall constitutes the third of the great houses of the Peak after Chatsworth ★ and Haddon ★ , although it is not so well known. Perhaps, in part, this is because of its location in the far west of the Park, the grounds themselves forming part of the boundary. It was home for 600 years to the Piers Legh family before they handed it over to the National Trust in 1946. They greatly altered the existing house in 1570 and it was around this Elizabethan structure that, in the eighteenth century, they commissioned the Venetian architect, Leoni, to design a new building. What emerged was a mansion in classic Palladian style, particularly impressive when viewed from the south.

The Hall was further enlarged in the nineteenth century with additions by Wyatt. Some of the most notable features inside are the superb carvings in the saloon and a large clock collection. The grounds are just as important an attraction, however, and the Hall lies in 1300 acres of attractive parkland containing a fine herd of red and fallow deer. There are bicycles for those wishing to explore the park extensively.

Magpie Mine (119) (SK 1768) ⅓ mile S of Sheldon

The assembly of ruined buildings on this lonely moor are the best-preserved remains of a nineteenth-century lead mine in Britain, and a stroll around them is highly recommended. The mine is a major feature of **Tour 8,** which concentrates on the industrial archaeology of The Peak. The site is looked after jointly by the Park authority and the Peak District Mines Historical Society. Further information can be obtained from the Mining Museum at Matlock Bath ★ . As with most Derbyshire lead mines, the Magpie Mine has had a long and chequered history with repeated openings and closures. Flooding was always a problem and, although lead was worked here as early as 1740, it was not until the discovery of a rich vein in 1810 that the mine became very profitable. Flooding was counteracted by the installation of a large Newcomen type pump in 1824 but the profits were absorbed by legal disputes with neighbouring mines. The rivalry between Magpie miners and those at nearby Redsoil and Maypitt mines came to a head with the death in 1833 of three Redsoil miners, overcome by poisonous fumes deliberately created by some Magpie men in adjacent workings.

In 1864 the mine was taken over by a Sheffield businessman, John Fairburn, who planned to solve the flooding problem by digging a drainage tunnel — or 'sough' — towards the Wye. It took eight years to cut through the hard 'toadstone' basalt and crippled the mine financially.

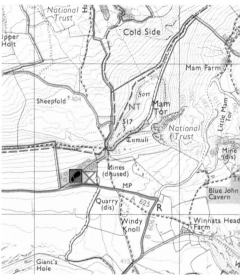

It also drained the springs supplying Sheldon, and waterwheels had to be built to pump water to the village. The mine closed once more in 1883 but there have been sporadic attempts to reopen it up to the 1950s, largely encouraged by high lead prices. Now the old boilerhouse chimneys and surrounding shafts and ruins remain as a fine monument to 'T'owd man'.

Mam Tor (110) (SK 1283) 1½ miles NW of Castleton

Mam Tor almost seals the western entrance of the Hope Valley. It forms the western end of the pronounced ridge to Lose Hill that effectively separates the White Peak to the south from the Vale of Edale and the Dark Peak to the north. Its nickname of 'Shivering Mountain' is well earned, as evidenced by the exposed vertical eastern face. The striped rocks reveal the cause of its instability, for the hill is composed of alternating layers of soft, impervious shale and porous harder grits that slide over one another when wet. This has had serious consequences for the main road at the foot of the hill. Originally constructed in 1812 for horse transport, it had to be largely rebuilt in 1945 only to slip again in 1977. Cracks had appeared during two dry summers and, when these were filled with rain during the following wet winter, conditions

A stroll to the top of Mam Tor is recommended, as there are 360 degree views from the top.

became very unstable and the road was forcibly diverted! The extent of the damage can best be seen from the summit or by those following the ridge on **Walk 4**.

The hill was probably named by the Celts and in their language meant 'mother mountain'. The same people are thought to have built the impressive Iron Age hillfort on the 1695-foot summit — the largest in the Peak. Unfortunately, part of its original 16 acres have disappeared down the hillside with the landslips but the pronounced ditch still remains. The fort was superbly sited — it included its own water supply — and would have held a commanding position for controlling the surrounding countryside. Research indicates that it may have supported a population of some size. The site itself seems to have been occupied much earlier, and fragments of pottery and deposits of charcoal have been dated to the Bronze Age.

A stroll to the top of the hill is recommended and could be added on to **Tours 6, 9**, and **10**. There is a well-waymarked path from the car park just off the A625 which is only a few hundred feet below the summit. Once there, you will probably be absorbed by the view which extends 360 degrees around the horizon. To the east and west is the spine of the ridge extending from Rushup Edge towards Lose Hill; to the south is a panoramic vista over Winnats Pass and the limestone plateau; while to the north is the brooding bulk of the Kinder Scout plateau and the highest land in the Peak.

Manifold Valley (119)

This beautiful valley is generally less well known than the nearby Dove, which is perhaps a little surprising for the rivers are close neighbours, rising within a mile of each other on Axe Edge and flowing south-eastwards in roughly parallel courses. In its upper reaches the Manifold flows across relatively soft shales and grits and forms a broad and shallow valley. Just below Hulme End, however, its character changes dramatically as it reaches the limestone. From here until it joins the Dove at Ilam, the scenery is superb with the huge, incised meanders that are supposed to have given the river its name. The Manifold and its tributary, the Hamps, are renowned for their disappearing act down swallets or 'shack holes' in their beds. There were amusing attempts in the last century to seal the swallets at Wetton Mill — needless to say unsuccessful — in an effort to maintain water supply from the Manifold. Coloured dye tests have shown that it reappears in the grounds at Ilam Hall some twenty-four hours later.

The Manifold is also notable for its caves, and there is evidence that these were in use from as early as Paleolithic times. The largest of these is Thor's Cave, visited on **Walk 6**. This is a most spectacular sight with its dramatic 60-foot high entrance some 250 feet above the valley floor. Archaeologists discovered a number of finds, including a Neolithic skeleton and a Roman coin. Nearby Elderbush Cave has yielded Paleolithic tools and animal bones, while Ossom's Cave, just upstream at Wetton Mill, is known to have been used for the working of flints. As well as providing shelter, the caves were used for

concealment, and an excavation at Beeston Tor in 1924 discovered forty-nine Saxon coins, gold rings, and silver brooches that were most likely hidden from the greedy gaze of the Vikings.

The lack of space in the steep, narrow valley meant that villages had to establish themselves on the plateau above the river. None is of any size, despite the arrival of the Leek and Manifold Light Railway in 1904. It followed a delightful route along the Manifold and Hamps valleys from Hulme End to Waterhouses but was conceived mainly as a goods line carrying raw materials, coal, and milk for the Ecton creamery. The locomotives on this unusual narrow-gauge railway were modelled on an Indian design, and today the whole package would make a wonderful tourist attraction. It was uneconomic, however, and ran for just thirty years. It has not disappeared without trace, though, for some of the old station buildings remain at Hulme End and the track bed has been tarmacked to form the Manifold Trail. The valley between Wetton Mill and Thor's Cave is explored on **Walk 6**. Motorists visit the valley on **Tours 1, 2, 4, 7**, and **9**.

Matlock and Matlock Bath (119) (SK 3060)

Although they share the same name and are virtually continuous, Matlock and Matlock Bath are two rather differing communities with one an ordinary town catering for the everyday needs of its residents and the other geared very much towards tourists. The development of both places was closely associated with the discovery of a local supply of thermal spring water but neither developed fully into a spa town and they have since diverged in appearance and function.

Although, today, Matlock is generally regarded as one town, it is actually made up of a number of separate hamlets that became established at various times and which merged later largely because of the development that occurred at the end of the nineteenth century. The site of the original village lies at the foot of the hill below

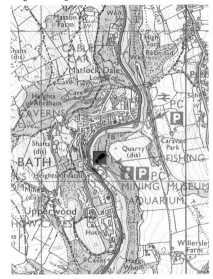

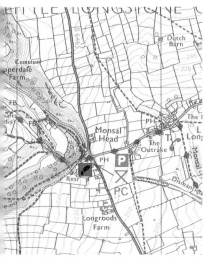

Above: *An old station, found on the Monsal Trail. The Trail runs from Blackwell Mill Junction in lovely Cheedale* (below).

built in 1863. This industrial intrusion into the dale was greatly lamented by John Ruskin who in his now famous outburst commented: 'The valley is gone and the Gods with it, and now every fool in Buxton can be in Bakewell in half an hour, end every fool in Bakewell at Buxton; which you think a lucrative process of exchange — you Fools Everywhere.'

Public attitudes have changed over time and now the viaduct and the track bed are a major feature of the Peak. The line closed in 1968 but, after twelve years of negotiation with British Rail, it was purchased by the Park and converted into the Monsal Trail between Blackwell Mill Junction in Chee Dale and Coombs Road Viaduct just south of Bakewell ★ . It is possible, however, that steam trains may once again thunder along the valley for there are plans by Peak Rail of Buxton ★ to reopen the line for the old locomotives. The viewpoint is included on **Tours 1** and **3** and the stroll is strongly recommended.

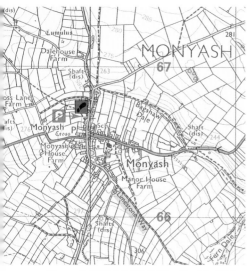

Monyash (119) (SK 1566) 4¹/₂ miles W of Bakewell

Glancing at the map, it would be hard to explain why this village should occupy a somewhat isolated position almost 900 feet up on the dry limestone plateau. A visit reveals all, however, for the Monyash lies at a spring line between the limestone and a localised patch of clay, and it clusters around its one remaining mere. The stone wall surrounding the pond was built to exclude animals from the precious water supply. The nearby well is dressed annually at the beginning of June. The church was founded in the late twelfth century and may seem over-large for this small community, but Monyash was once an important market centre, receiving its charter in 1340. The cross on the green, with its medieval base, is the only visible evidence of the once weekly market.

Some local industries did develop in the village but, by and large, Monyash depended on the typical dual activities of agriculture and lead mining. It held some importance as a mining centre, for a Barmote court was held in the village to settle local disputes. The village also had strong Quaker traditions, and John Gratton, an early Quaker, was born here in the seventeenth century. The industries and activities have faded away but have left a peaceful, attractive village that the visitor is recommended to explore on a stroll. This could be added on to **Tour 8**.

Parwich (119) (SK 1854) 1¹/₂ miles NE of Tissington

Lying just inside the south-eastern boundary of the Park, Parwich is a large limestone village which grew up around its green. It contains some attractive buildings but the village tends to be dominated by the prominent church spire. This dates from 1873, when the original Norman church was completely rebuilt. A tympanum from the earlier building was preserved, however, and now lies over the northern doorway. Parwich Hall backs on to the steep slopes of Parwich Hill and is particularly notable for its brick and stone construction — an unusual combination for Peak buildings. It was completed in 1747 on top of foundations of an earlier sixteenth-century house and may have been in-

fluenced by the Hall at Great Longstone, also built in brick and finished in the same year. Parwich is included on **Tour 2**.

Peak Forest (119) (SK 1179) 3¼ miles NW of Tideswell

The village name derives from its ancient location near the centre of the Royal Forest of the Peak, an area of some 40 square miles set aside initially by the Norman kings as an exclusive royal hunting ground. Despite its title, the Forest was not heavily wooded but mainly open country that supported wolves, wild boar, and deer. It remained a significant feature of the Peak landscape for 500 years until its official disafforestation in 1674.

The village held some importance in the administration of the Forest but is better known for the clandestine marriages conducted in the church. These earned the village its nickname of 'the Gretna Green of the Peak' where marriage licences were issued with no awkward questions — for a small fee to the church incumbent, of course. This was possible because the church was built as a private chapel and was therefore outside any episcopal jurisdiction. Up to sixty run-away marriages were conducted each year, the last occurring in 1804. In fact, everything about the church flaunted authority, for it was originally built by the Countess of Devonshire during a Commonwealth ban on church building in 1657 and, furthermore, dedicated rather provocatively to King Charles the Martyr.

Eldon Hole, just to the north of the village, is the most impressive open pot hole of the Peak, long held to be bottomless and one of the tradi-

The scale of Hen Cloud makes it a very popular place for climbers.

tional 'Seven Wonders'. It is actually only about 200 feet deep, less than half the depth of the Giant's Hole a mile further north. **Tour 4** passes through the village.

The Roaches and Ramshaw Rocks (118 and 119) (SK 0063 — trig point) 2 miles NW of Upper Hulme

These impressive rocks guard the south-western edge of the Peak and mark the beginning — or end — of the sterner, upland country of northern Britain. They form the western arm of the horseshoe of grit that surrounds the White Peak but, in contrast to the darker gritstone of the east, the rocks have a pleasant reddish hue. They are seen to stunning effect from the Morridge road to the east, included on **Tour 7**, from where it is easy to trace the V formation made by the Roaches and Hen Cloud to the west and Ramshaw Rocks to the east.

The rocks face opposite directions and have been greatly folded into a syncline, with the grit forming the upper edges or rim that rises to 1657 feet. In some places the strata have been tilted by as much as 40 degrees, seen to best effect in the crazy angles of the jagged Ramshaw Rocks. One such formation is the famous 'Winking Eye Rock' seen from **Tours 4** and **7**. The centre of the basin was partly filled with coal-bearing measures, and the boggy area of Goldsitch Moss was once a productive coalfield, albeit on a small and local scale. The Roaches' unusual name probably derives from the French word for rocks — *roches*. The grit

The spectacular view towards Hen Cloud from the Roaches.

75

From the Morridge road, included on Tour 7, it is easy to trace the V formation of the Roaches and Hen Cloud to the west (top) and Ramshaw Rocks to the east (below).

rises in two tiers here, first forming the ledge of Five Clouds and then the summit ridge of the Roaches themselves. Hen Cloud lies isolated to the south-east and, with its abrupt western edge, somewhat resembles a greatly misplaced Rock of Gibraltar. It is a pity that the climate does not match its appearance!

The coarse gritstone forms excellent climbing country and walkers are quite likely to see brightly clad figures clinging precariously to the steep rock faces. They are in good company, for several well-known climbers began their careers here. There are superb views from the summits particularly to the south where, on a sunny day, the eye is drawn automatically to the glinting waters of Tittesworth Reservoir. The rocks are visited on **Tours 4** and **7**, and further explored on **Walk 11**.

Robin Hood's Stride (119) (SK 2262) 1 mile W of Birchover
From a distance, the twin turrets of this curious gritstone formation resemble chimneys on the roof line of some stone mansion. For this reason, it is known alternatively as Mock Beggar's Hall. Its other name was taken from the distance between the two highest tors which, at almost 70 feet, was said to be the length of Robin Hood's stride! At the foot of Cratcliffe Tor just to the east near an ancient yew tree lies the Hermit's Cave, wherein some medieval recluse carved a bench, a lamp niche, and a crucifix out of the stone. The entrance is railed off now but these features can just be made out from the en-

trance. Their date is uncertain but it is known that the cave was occupied in 1549, because the resident is noted in the records of Haddon Hall for supplying ten rabbits.

Archaeological remains close by show that this site held considerable importance. Just to the north-east of Robin Hood's Stride is the Nine Stones Circle, a Bronze Age structure now reduced to four monoliths. These are among the tallest stones in the region — one has been measured at 11 feet 8 inches — and, unlike Arbor Low, these have remained erect. About half-a-mile to the north-west lies the Iron Age hillfort known as Castle Ring, a large encampment partially built upon, and damaged by, ploughing. This lay close to the route of the Portway, an ancient track that came north from Wirksworth ★, past the cave and tors, across Harthill Moor to Alport ★ and down to the Wye at Ashford ★. There are also good views from the tor summits and a stroll is highly recommended.

Rowsley (119) (SK 2565) 3 miles SE of Bakewell
Rowsley stands right on the Park's eastern boundary where the A6 enters from the south. Of greater historical significance, however, is its situation at the confluence of the Wye and the Derwent — two major Peakland rivers. The five-arched, seventeenth-century bridge lies just upstream of this point and is easily missed by most motorists just speeding through on the main road. Rowsley gained further importance with the arrival of the Midland line from Derby and, for twenty years, formed its northern railhead until the route was extended through the Wye Valley to Buxton ★ in 1860.

The village contains some fine buildings, almost all of which are owned by the Duke of Rutland. Of particular note is the Peacock Hotel, one of the best known in the Peak District, and which was originally built as a private house in 1652 before conversion to an inn early in the nineteenth century. Caudwell Mill is another impressive construction, built beside the Wye

in 1874 and still using water power up to 1978. It has since been restored, and the roller milling machinery installed early this century is now fully operational. It also houses a variety of craftsmen including a glass blower, a wood turner, a clock maker, and a potter. Their products are for sale in the craft shop, and the public may also view the mill machinery. Rowsley is included on **Tours 8** and **9**.

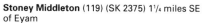

Stoney Middleton (119) (SK 2375) 1¼ miles SE of Eyam

The village has an impressive setting between towering limestone cliffs which rise vertically from the floor of the valley. It was at one time a centre for boot and shoe manufacture, but it is immediately evident that quarrying and mining have been vital to the village, and the countryside roundabout is littered with disused lead mines and old limestone quarries. There are two large quarries beside the main road just to the west where they have eaten into the limestone, but most of the employment locally is obtained from the fluorspar works high up on the moorland behind the village.

The A623 was first built in 1840 as a turnpike, and the original tollhouse can still be seen beside the road — now selling fish and chips! Other interesting features are situated away from the main road, including an unusual and rare octagonal church. Behind this is the Jacobean Hall, and in the delightful and secluded square are two wells which are dressed in late July. Above the village is Lover's Leap, site in 1765 of an attempted suicide when Hannah Baddaley threw herself over the cliff. She may possibly be credited with the first parachute for her descent was sufficiently slowed by her billowing skirts and some protruding bramble bushes to enable her to survive the fall!

Known as the 'Cathedral of the Peak', Tideswell parish church (left) is also famed for its superb brasses (above).

Tideswell (119) (SK 1575) 6 miles E of Buxton

Tideswell is dominated by its magnificent parish church, justly praised as the 'Cathedral of the Peak'. It was built from the wealth gained by the production of wool and lead, and constructed in the relatively short time span between about 1300 and 1370. This is rare in English churches and lends the building a certain unity of appearance and style. Its construction spanned two architectural periods, however, and there is a marked difference between the flowing tracery of the Decorated period in the transept and east windows, and the more regular lines of the solid

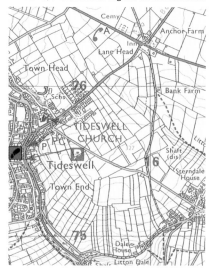

tower, built later in the Perpendicular fashion. The spacious chancel receives considerable light from the tall windows at its eastern and its western ends, and has a wonderful lofty and airy feel. The church is also famed for its superb brasses, one of which — that to John Foljambe in the late fourteenth century — is among the earliest in Derbyshire. The nineteenth-century wood carving is also worthy of note, and this reflects the long-standing tradition of this craft in the village.

The rest of Tideswell tends to be overshadowed by the church but there is much more to see in this attractive village. There are lots of examples of the vernacular architecture among the small alleyways, and several outstanding individual buildings. Among these are the vicarage and library near the church and the George Hotel, an old coaching inn with Venetian windows dating from the eighteenth century. Tideswell is quite a busy place today with a wide variety of shops and services. It has long been an important trading centre, and received its market charter in 1250. It prospered with the lead and wool industries in the fourteenth century but declined thereafter, thus preserving the church in its medieval glory. The village is visited on **Tours 1** and **6** and a stroll around the village is strongly recommended.

Tissington and Fenny Bentley (119) (SK 1752)
1½ miles SW of Parwich

Tissington is held by many to be the prettiest village in the Peak. It certainly contains many of the features regarded as typical of the English village — a green, a pond, a church, a splendid manor house, and attractive cottages, here set back spaciously behind strips of grass. Many of the houses were rebuilt at about the middle of the last century by the Fitzherbert family, who have been predominant in the village since Elizabethan times. The original manor house stood next to the church but, early in the seventeenth century, the Fitzherberts built the imposing Hall, just across the road, and took up resi-

The imposing Tissington Hall was built by the Fitzherbert family — a family that has been predominant in the village since Elizabethan times.

dence here around 1610. The building has been extended twice during the Georgian period and earlier this century.

The village is best known for its well dressing, and Tissington is traditionally the first place to decorate its wells each season, on Ascension Day. The spring water here preserved the health of many of the villagers during the Black Death in the fourteenth century and is known to have continued flowing during a drought in 1615. This may explain why the tradition is particularly strong in the village and why it can claim one of the earliest recorded accounts of the custom, in 1758. For centuries there had been five wells but a sixth, Children's Well, was introduced for the first time in 1982 at the whim of Yorkshire TV, who wished to film children involved in the process of dressing. Despite the relative lack of flowers so early in the season and a strict rule regulating the use of only natural materials, the wells are a spectacular site and attract thousands of visitors.

To the south lies the car park and former railway station, now part of the Tissington Trail. One-and-a-half miles further to the south lies Fenny Bentley, the Peak Park's most southerly village. In the church is the curious tomb of Thomas Beresford, his wife and their twenty-one children — all wrapped in shrouds. Their fifteenth-century moated manor house with its massive square tower can be seen briefly from the A515.

It is recommended that the visitor takes a stroll around Tissington — further information about the village can be obtained from the

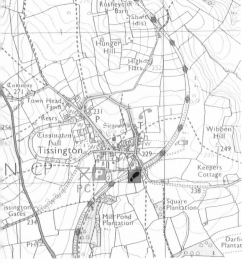

It is easy to see why the conical peak of Shutlingsloe is nicknamed the 'Matterhorn of the Peak'.

church. Both Tissington and Fenny Bentley are included on **Tour 9**.

Wildboarclough (118) (SJ 9868) 2½ miles NE of Danebridge

Confined by the steep-sided valley of the Clough Brook, this tiny village is built largely from the local, warm-pink gritstone. Its name is romantic and evocative but the last wild boar is thought to have been hunted here in the fifteenth century, and the village is known more correctly as Crag. It may seem quiet and insignificant today but the Clough Brook powered three silk mills here in the eighteenth century. One of these — Crag Mill — later made carpets for the Great Exhibition of 1851. It was demolished in 1958 but the administration block remained and was converted into what must have been the largest sub-post office in the country. This has now closed and the village is a sheltered backwater nestling under the shapely conical peak of Shutlingsloe, nicknamed the 'Matterhorn of the Peak'. There are very fine views of the whole area from its 1659-foot peak including the Mersey Plain and Jodrell Bank.

A stroll around the village incorporating the old post office is recommended and could be incorporated with **Tour 4**.

The old post office, Wildboarclough.

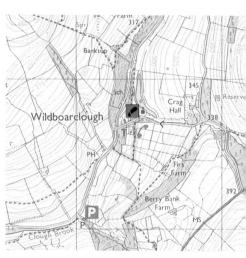

Winnats Pass (110) (SK 1382) 1 mile W of Castleton

Limestone outcrops and caves dot the sides of this spectacular steep gorge and it is now a designated Site of Special Scientific Interest (SSSI). It was bought by the National Trust in 1944 and used to be the main turnpike road until this was diverted along the easier gradients under Mam Tor ★. The landslip of 1977 closed this latter route and light traffic now uses the road through the Pass. The narrow gap tends to funnel the wind, and its alternative name of Windgates is appropriate enough during the winter months.

The Pass is a channel that breached the ancient reef surrounding the shallow waters of the Carboniferous lagoon. The lagoon lay to the south and west, and the steep slopes above Castleton and Treak Cliff represent the old fore reef that plunged sharply into the deeper waters of the open sea to the north. The scenery is fascinating and well worth exploring on a stroll. The Pass is included on **Tours 3, 6,** and **9**.

'The Dream Cave', Treak Cliff Cavern (Derbyshire Countryside Ltd).

Winster (119) (SK 2460) 1 mile S of Birchover Winster was an important lead mining centre, and many of the handsome houses and cottages of this attractive village were built during the heyday of the local industry in the eighteenth century. There are earlier buildings, though, notably the seventeenth-century Dower House at the western end of the main street and the sixteenth-century Market Hall which juts out into the road in the middle of the village. The Market Hall has a sixteenth-century ground floor — originally open as at Bakewell ★ , but since filled in — and a brick upper storey dating from the seventeenth century. It is owned by the National Trust and houses an information centre and shop. It represents something of a landmark for, when the National Trust bought it in 1906, it was their first acquisition in the Peak District. Winster has several traditions including morris dancing, an annual Pancake race, and a Wakes week at the end of June.

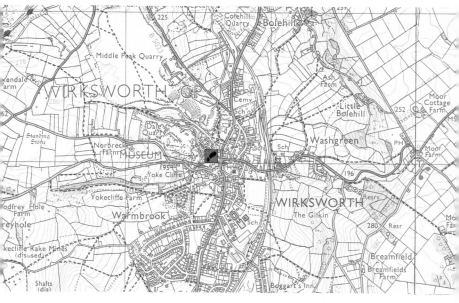

It is well worth taking a stroll around the village and it is included on **Tour 2**.

Wirksworth (119) (SK 2854) 1¾ miles S of Cromford

Wirksworth lies at the south-eastern edge of the Peak Park at the head of the Ecclesbourne Valley. It is an ancient township that held great importance for the lead mining industry from Roman times and, according to some historians, it may be the site of 'Lutudarum' — the centre of Roman lead mining activities. A Barmote Court, with its Barmaster and jury of twelve 'miners', still meets twice a year in Moot Hall. This is the oldest industrial court in the country,

known to have operated since at least 1266. Inside the building is the bronze dish used to measure the amount of lead ore, made in 1513 with a capacity of 14 pints.

Wirksworth declined greatly with the demise of lead mining, but recently much effort has gone into restoring the fabric of the village. Many attractive old buildings have been restored as part of a comprehensive civic trust project and are worth seeking out among the side streets. These radiate out from the slanting market square in the middle of the village. Nearby is the Heritage Centre with informative and unusual displays which provide fascinating insights into the historical customs and lifestyle of the villagers. The church is also an interest-

The oldest industrial court in the country still operates twice a year at Moot Hall, Wirksworth.

Fine Saxon carvings can be found in the church at Wirksworth.

It is well worth climbing the hill to look down on the village of Wirksworth.

ing place to visit although it may be hard to find at first. It is concealed behind rows of shops and reached through narrow alleyways — even the tower is virtually hidden from the village centre. It stands at the centre of a circular close that is pleasantly peaceful after the noise and hubbub of the adjacent main street. The thirteenth- to fourteenth-century tower is topped by a small spire that looks ridiculously undersized and makes Wirksworth church unmistakeable. There was a church here in Saxon times and the building is famous for its outstanding stone carvings of the period, seen on the walls inside. Included among these Saxon treasures are a coffin lid dating from the late seventh century and probably the Peak's earliest Christian monument.

Wirksworth dresses nine wells from the Saturday before the late Spring Bank Holiday. The custom started in 1827 when they were known as Tap Dressings, to celebrate the installation of a water supply. In early September the annual ceremony of Clypping — or embracing — the church takes place. Wirksworth is full of character and it is worth climbing the hill above the village to look down over the irregular roof lines and the distinctive church spire. A stroll is highly recommended and could be incorporated with **Tour 8**.

Youlgreave (119) (SK 2164) 2³⁄₄ miles S of Bakewell

The village name has a variety of spellings and may have originated from the Saxon *Auldgroove* — which means 'old mine' — and miners hereabouts are called 'groovers'. The locals refer to the place as 'Pommy', however. This large attractive village has grown in linear fashion along a shelf of fairly level ground above the steep banks of the River Bradford, which here forms a delightful valley reached by numerous alleyways from the south side of the main street. Lead mining was important and many of the cottages were built by mine workers.

The church is second only in size to that of Tideswell ★ and is situated in the the main street — the imposing fifteenth-century Perpendicular tower almost seeming to block the road. It contains much Norman work, including the nave and a unique double font — 'acquired' from Elton church in 1833. There are several monuments of interest, most notably the alabaster tomb and effigy of Thomas Cockayne, who died in 1488.

This is a village of some character with some fine old buildings. Among these are the seventeenth-century Old Hall and Old Hall Farm, some Georgian houses near the church and the youth hostel — a nineteenth-century building originally constructed as a shop for the local Co-operative Society. Opposite the hostel is an oval stone tank installed in 1829 as part of a public water supply system by the village's own

water company — Youlgreave is one of the few English villages to have its own water undertaking. The tank is officially called Conduit Head but is referred to locally as The Fountain and receives soft water from a spring outside the village. In celebration of the provision of a water supply, it was the site of the first well dressing in 1829 and marked the beginning of an annual custom that now decorates five wells at the end of June. Youlgreave is renowned for its exceptionally high standard of dressing and villagers have put on displays elsewhere in England and in Germany.

Youlgreave is included on **Tour 1** and it is recommended that the visitor take a stroll around the village. **Walk 1** also passes through the village.

The Arbor Low stone circle near Youlgreave.

Tour 1
The Limestone Dales

54 miles. This tour of the White Peak passes through some of the most spectacular limestone scenery, including the gorges of the Wye, the Lathkill and the Dove. It also includes the memorable villages of Ashford in the Water, Tideswell, Alstonefield and Ilam, and a full day will be required if all features are to be properly explored. The tour begins in Bakewell but, for those approaching the Peak from Ashbourne, it could equally well start on the A515 near Tissington.

From the centre of Bakewell ★, take the A6 north towards Buxton ★, passing Victoria Mill with its large iron wheel on the right near the edge of the town. Turn right off the A6 (**A**) then left into the attractive village of Ashford-in-the-Water ★, following the B6465 to Monsal Head ★. The Monsal Head viaduct is one of the Peak District's most famous landmarks, and the stroll across it is highly recommended. Car parking for the view and stroll is on the

The almost surreal atmosphere given by the large numbers of dry stone walls near Litton.

left just before the Monsal Head Hotel.

Turn left out of the car park, then left again in front of the hotel (**B**), and take the minor road to Cressbrook. Go past the magnificent Cressbrook Mill which is now sadly in a state of disrepair and, at the fork, bear right to Litton ★. The road now climbs on to the plateau, with typical open, rolling scenery. Where the road forks, bear right (**C**). The extent of the dry stone walling in this area is quite astonishing and lends an almost surreal atmosphere to the landscape.

Turn left in Litton, then fork right at the memorial, following the road straight on into Tideswell ★. Turn left and follow the B6049 through the village and down beautiful Tideswell Dale with its limestone crags, into Millers Dale, where the spectacular Chee Dale Walk (**Walk 12**) starts nearby. Pass beneath the viaduct, which used to carry the Peak Line, connecting Matlock ★ with Buxton before it was closed in 1968. The old course now carries the Monsal Trail, a popular route for walkers and cyclists.

Climb back to the open country, then at the junction with the A6 (**D**), turn right, then left after half a mile on to the A5270. The vast scale of the area's largest limestone quarry can be seen ahead. At the junction with the A515 turn left towards Ashbourne. Note the cutting in the hillside on the right where the Tissington Trail, a

Scale 1:250 000 or ¼ INCH to 1 MILE

former railway, cuts through a hillside; this joins the High Peak Trail which soon passes beneath the road.

Turn right (**E**) on the B5054 to Hartington ★. There is a picnic area on the left just before the bridge carrying the High Peak Trail; an old signal box, complete with control levers, still remains. Follow the B5054 through Hartington towards Warslow. Turn left (**F**) towards Alstonefield ★ by the Manifold Valley Hotel. The road climbs towards an impressive line of peaks, almost 'alpine' by Peak District standards. When Derbyshire basked in tropical sunshine some 300 million years ago, these knolls were actually reefs, poking upwards from the floor of a shallow sea. We see them today because they are harder and therefore less easily eroded than the surrounding limestone.

In the largely unspoilt village of Alstonefield ★ turn right at the white hand pump and follow the signs through Hope ★ and Stanshope to llam ★ and Dovedale

★. Turn left at the monument at the monument in llam, and left again by the Isaac Walton Hotel into Dovedale and into the car park from where you may take a stroll — a pleasant although often busy spot in this best-known part of the Dove Valley. Return to the junction, turn left, and follow the road through Thorpe, heading towards Tissington ★.

Turn left (**G**) on to the A515, and at Newhaven turn right, signposted Cromford ★, then left to Middleton, passing Friden brickworks — an unusual feature in the Peaks, but dependent on local deposits of silica sand for the manufacture of fire-bricks.

Turn right (**H**) and pass through Middleton and on into Youlgreave ★, where there is a pleasant stroll down to the river. Towards the end of the village turn left opposite the church and descend into Lathkill Dale ★, turning right at the junction and crossing Conksbury Bridge, and continuing back into Bakewell.

Tour 2
Dovedale and the Manifold Valley

*42 miles. This route passes through the beautiful White Peak valleys of the Dove and the Manifold with their enticing woodlands and spectacular rock features. Using narrow, minor roads it also goes through the relatively unknown villages of Brassington, Winster, and Wensley, as well as the popular village of Hartington. The short distance and quiet roads make it an ideal route for cyclists, and walkers may wish to try **Walks 2** or **6** to make it a day's outing. Motorists approaching from*

The packhorse bridge made famous as Viators Bridge in Izaac Walton's The Compleat Angler.

*Buxton could take the A515 Ashbourne road and join the route just north of Newhaven (**F**), while those approaching on the A515 from Ashbourne could start from point (**D**).*

Take the A6 south (marked Derby) from Matlock ★ and follow it as far as Cromford ★ ; then turn right (**A**) on to the B5036 towards Wirksworth ★ . The road now climbs out of the Derwent Valley and, for those wanting an early break, good views can be obtained of Matlock and the surrounding area from the pleasant gritstone outcrop of Black Rocks, which can be reached by taking the left turn to the car park and picnic site. About 200 yards past the turning to the picnic site (**B**), however, turn right on to the B5035 towards Middleton. Go straight on at the crossroads and, after about 1 mile turn right at the next

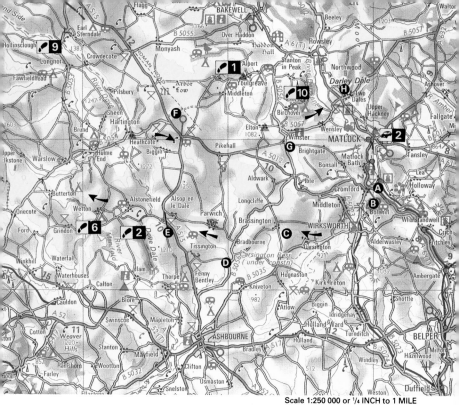

Scale 1:250 000 or ¼ INCH to 1 MILE

crossroads to Brassington ★.

Turn left into Brassington (**C**), then sharp right in the village towards the 'Miners Arms', and past the church. Continue through Bradborne to the B5056. Turn right (**D**) and, after a mile, turn left to Parwich ★ — a village which improves after a somewhat unprepossessing start. Turn left down a narrow lane to Alsop, passing along a pretty valley so typical of the southern Peak, through Alsop to the A515.

Turn left (**E**) and after ½ mile turn right to Milldale descending an intimate, wooded valley and forking left after crossing the Dove. Milldale has a tea shop, and parking and is an excellent spot to break the journey. The energetically inclined may wish to savour the delights of the Dove and the surrounding countryside by tackling **Walk 2** which starts here.

Follow the road up the valley to Hopedale, then turn left and follow the signs to Wetton, passing through the village and taking the lane to Wettonmill. A stunning view of the Manifold valley ★ soon unfolds — look out on the left for the dramatic arch of Thor's Cave, one of the wonders of the Peak, and visited in **Walk 6** which starts in Wetton.

In the valley floor the road splits; take the right fork which is actually a section of the Manifold Way, once the course of the Leek and Manifold Light Railway which oper-

ated in 1904-1934, but is now a walking/cycling/horse riding route, and in parts a road. Wetton Mill is also a good spot for a break, with car parking and refreshments available at the mill.

Continue along the Manifold way, through the tunnel and bear right to Ecton ★. The valley side on the right is riddled with the remains of a once very profitable copper mine belonging to the Dukes of Devonshire. During the eighteenth century it was the largest in Europe and, at its acme, employed about 300 people. Follow the signs for Hulme End, passing through Ecton and Westside, before turning left at a T-junction, and continuing to a main road.

Turn right on the B5054 into Hartington ★, around which there is a stroll. Follow the road through the village to the junction with the A515. Turn right (**F**), and left after a mile on to the A5012 marked Matlock. Where the road bears right, go straight on to Winster ★ and, at the junction (**G**), turn left, then right after 100 yards and descend into the village, where there is a pleasant stroll. Turn right on the main street to Darley Dale ★. As you leave the village, look across the valley on the left to Stanton Moor, an isolated, flat-topped, gritstone hill covered with Bronze Age relics and explored in **Walk 10**. Follow the B5057 through Wensley to the A6, then turn right (**H**) back to Matlock.

Tour 3
Castleton and the Eastern Edges

39 miles. This is a tour through the heart of the Peak, taking in its two most famous villages—Castleton and Bakewell. It winds northwards from Baslow beneath the impressive eastern gritstone edges, where there are good views, through the interesting village of Hathersage, before returning to the limestone during a climb through spectacular Winnats Pass. It returns to Bakewell via Monsal Head and the pretty village of Ashford-in-the-Water. Although the route begins in Bakewell, those approaching from Sheffield on the A625 could join the route at The Fox House Inn (B), (SK 267803), and those approaching on the A625 from the west could join it at Castleton.

From the centre of Bakewell ★, follow the A619 signposted to Chesterfield and, at the roundabout in Baslow ★, turn left on the A623 to Calver ★ (there are strolls in both of these Derwent villages). Follow the road through Calver to the traffic lights and turn right on to the B6001 Hathersage ★ road. After ¼ mile turn right (A) on the

Froggatt Edge, forming an almost continuous wall running north from Baslow.

B6054 marked Sheffield. Cross the Derwent and climb through Froggatt — there are good views of Froggatt Edge ahead, one of many similar edges (popular with rock climbers) that form an almost continuous wall running north from Baslow. Beyond them to the east, remote and wild moors cloaked in grasses and heather slope gently down to the suburbs of Sheffield and Chesterfield. Emerge from the woodland on to the moor, then turn left towards Sheffield at the first junction, and go straight on at the second.

At the junction by The Fox House (B) turn left on to the A625 to Hathersage. This particularly attractive section of Burbage Moor — like many of the gritstone moors — has interesting, weather-worn rock sculptures such as the Toads Mouth Rock. A magnificent panorama of hills and the broad Derwent Valley unfolds — aptly known as 'Surprise View' — as the sharp right-hand bend is negotiated. The A625 descends into Hathersage where a worthwhile stroll visits Little John's grave among other things; this begins from the car park reached by turning left by the telephone box and following Crossland Road for several hundred yards.

Leave the car park and return to the junction with the A625. Turn left, then sharp right on the bend towards the Church. The road now climbs the very pretty Dale Bottom, towards the high moors. Take the turning on the left to Ladybower (C) and pass beneath Stanage

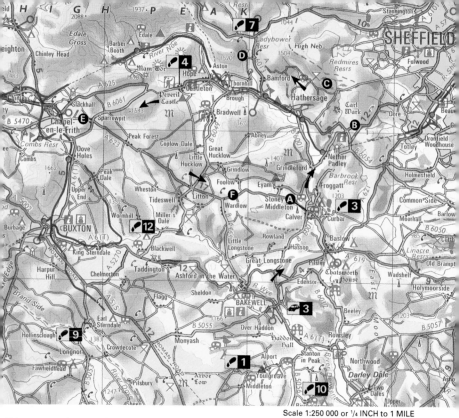

Scale 1:250 000 or ¼ INCH to 1 MILE

Edge — an impressive 2-mile gritstone edge very popular with climbers and hang glider pilots — and turn right after ½ mile, continuing to follow the signs to Ladybower. At the junction with the A6013 (**D**), turn left and go through Bamford ★ to the junction with the A625; turn right, passing through Hope ★ into Castleton ★ — an excellent place to stop and take a stroll. **Walk 4**, a circuit of the surrounding hills including Mam Tor ★, starts from the car park and those interested in some subterranean exploration will be spoilt for choice because there are four caverns to choose from within a mile of the village.

Turn right out of the car park and, at the junction, bear left up magnificent Winnats Pass ★ (signposted Speedwell Cavern) — an interesting stroll for the energetic. At the junction at the top turn left on to the B6061 to Sparrowpit, and at the junction with the A623 (**E**) turn left towards Chesterfield. The A623 crosses the rolling hills of the limestone plateau, passing through the hamlet of Peak Forest ★. Continue past the Tideswell ★ turning, and look out for the craggy outline of Peter's Stone on the right at the head of Cressbrook Dale.

At the junction with the B6465 (**F**), turn right to Ashford-in-the-Water ★, passing by Monsal Head where there is a car park next to the hotel — the starting point for a spectacular and energetic stroll across the Monsal Viaduct. Continue into Ashford-in-the-Water, where there is also an absorbing stroll around this beautiful riverside village, and turn right, then left on to the A6 back into Bakewell.

Tour 4
Buxton and the Western Moors

36 miles. The land to the south-west of Buxton is wild and sparsely populated gritstone moorland. This tour follows twisting and undulating minor roads across the distinctive valleys of the Goyt, Clough Brook, Dane, Manifold, and Dove. It also passes through tiny hamlets, with such intriguing names as Bottom-of-the-Oven, Wildboarclough, and Wincle.

From the town centre car park by the viaduct, follow the signs for Leek (A53) at first, until the signs for Whaley Bridge (A5004) appear. Follow this road uphill out of Buxton ★ and, at the hilltop (**A**), turn left along a minor road to the Goyt Valley. The road now descends into wild and sparsely populated country, and views of Fernilee and Errwood reservoirs unfold. Fernilee was built in 1938, followed by Errwood some thirty years later. It is hard to imagine that, before the reservoirs, this valley had a thriving farming community and some light industry, including a gunpowder factory employing 120 men before World War I. Now it is the preserve of walkers and, on Errwood, dinghy sailors. The upper reaches of the Goyt Valley are explored in **Walk 8**. Cross the dam and turn right (**B**) to Kettleshulme, climbing on to open moorland, before descending into the Todd valley. Turn left around the unusual church and proceed to the next junction and turn left to Lamaload.

Go straight on across the A537 (**C**) and follow the signs to Wildboarclough ★ , bearing right at the unmarked fork. Wildboarclough is a pleasant place to stop and take a stroll, and is overlooked by the shapely summit of Shutlingsloe, one of the best-known landmarks of the western Peak. Carry on from Wildboarclough and follow the signs to Wincle. Go straight on across the A54 (**D**). In Wincle turn left by the church towards Swythamley, following the road past the 'Ship Inn' in Danebridge, and crossing the attractive valley of the Dane. Go straight on at the next junction (**E**), along the lane where coaches are prohibited, then bear right towards Leek at the next junction, and after a mile bear left to Meerbrook. A spectacular view of the serrated crests of Hen Cloud and The Roaches ★ comes into view, with Titteswell reservoir in the foreground. In Meerbrook (**F**), turn left to Roach Grange, or go straight on across the reservoir to the visitor centre where refreshments are available.

The road climbs steeply towards the Roaches and, after Roach Grange, turn right to Upper Hulme, passing beneath the magnificent wooded slopes below the ridge. The summit is traversed in **Walk 11**, which begins from the lay-by near the end of the ridge. Turn left (**G**) on to the A53 and pass the impressive slabs of Ramshaw Rocks ★ . Have you spotted the Winking Eye Rock? Turn right (**H**) to Longnor ★ , eventually crossing the infant Manifold, and then climbing the ridge into the village. This solid, workaday village is a good place for a stroll, and you can park in the market square opposite the junction. Return to the junction and turn right towards Buxton; cross the Dove and climb between the peaks of Chrome, Parkhouse and Hitter hills — once reefs beneath a shallow sea and now probably the White Peak's best known 'mountains'. **Walk 9**, beginning in nearby Hollinsclough, is an interesting circuit of Chrome Hill.

Over the brow of the hill, the quarry and the surrounding fields dusted with white fallout come as an unpleasant surprise. Continue past the quarry, then turn left on to the A515 back into Buxton.

Fernilee reservoir, built in 1938, was once a valley with a thriving farming community.

Scale 1:250 000 or ¼ INCH to 1 MILE

Tour 5
Glossop and the Northern Moors

52 miles. Reservoirs quenching the thirst of the great conurbations of Sheffield and Manchester are the main theme of this journey, because at least fifteen of them lie close to the route. From Glossop it climbs through typical moorland scenery as it crosses the 'Backbone of England' before descending through the Bradfields — quiet, interesting villages just a few miles from Sheffield, yet relatively unknown. From here the journey winds across lovely moorland to the Derwent reservoirs — the 'Lake District of the Peak'. The return to Glossop is via the A57 Snake Pass Road with its dramatic views of Kinder Scout. If you are thinking of attempting this route during the winter months, bear in mind that, in periods of bad weather, it is usually the first trans-Pennine route to close. The tour starts from Glossop, but for those approaching from Sheffield, the route could be joined either by taking the A616 to Langsett or the A57 to Moscar (F).

From the centre of Glossop ★ , take the B6105 Barnsley road (via Woodhead), and enter Longdendale ★ , a dark valley of undistinguished reservoirs and stark power lines overlooked by the wild splendours of Bleaklow ★ . Turn right (A) on to the A628, a very busy trans-Pennine route between Manchester and Sheffield. The scenery improves, however, as the road climbs to the summit of the Pennine backbone where views of the industrial eastern Pennine towns of Barnsley and Sheffield unfold. On the left you may see the Holme Moss television mast, and beyond it is the huge concrete tower of the Emley Moor transmitter. Standing some 1084 feet above the moor, it is the tallest concrete structure in Britain. Under certain conditions this slender tower pierces the clouds and its top may be seen poking above them — so unreal a sight is it that it may demand a second glance!

By the Flouch Inn (B), take the A616 right to Sheffield and turn right in Langsett towards Strines and Derwent Valley. Cross the dam and turn right towards Strines. Turn right (C) again to Strines and cross the attractive Ewden Beck and climb once more. Go past the first junction on the left to the delightfully named Wigtwizzle, then take the left fork to Bradfield ★ . Continue straight on at the cross roads and descend into High Bradfield ★ , a good place to stop for a stroll. At the junction by the telephone box (D), turn right and descend

Scale 1:250 000 or ¼ INCH to 1 MILE

Longdendale is overlooked by the wild splendour of Bleaklow.

steeply to Low Bradfield ★. Go around to the left of the sports field and take the Penistone and Strines road (right), then go straight on to Strines and Derwent Valley. At the junction (**E**) take the right fork to Midhopestones, then left at the next junction to the Derwent Valley The peculiar 50-foot high tower on the hillside to the left above the reservoir is 'Boots Folly', built in 1927 by Charles Boot of nearby Bent's House, using stone from demolished properties.

Turn right (**F**) to Glossop and descend this very pleasant stretch of the A57 to the Ladybower Reservoir. **Walk 7** starts from the lay-by alongside the reservoir and could provide a pleasant 2-hour interlude. For the less energetic, however, it is well worth turning right at the end of the bridge

spanning the reservoir and driving the 3 miles to Fairholmes ★, where there is a quiet picnic site and visitor centre and also a gentle stroll. **Walk 5** — a strenuous 5-hour moorland crossing to the rock pinnacles of Alport Castles ★ — also begins here.

Return to the A57 and continue to Glossop. The climb up to Snake Pass (no connection with the sinuous shape of the road but with the Cavendish Family Arms) is particularly attractive with splendid views of the bare northern flanks of Kinder Scout ★ on the left. The route climbs to the 1680-foot summit of Snake Pass before descending into Glossop.

Tour 6
The two sides of the Peak

48 miles. This route encompasses contrasting aspects of the Peakland scenery from the open, acid moorland of the Dark Peak, with its spectacular views across the Cheshire Plain, to the awesome gorges and verdant pastures of the White Peak. The settlements are of contrast too — from the industrialised townships of Whaley Bridge and Chapel-en-le-Frith to the famous tourist honeypots of Castleton, Eyam, Tideswell, and Buxton. The tour begins in Buxton, but those approaching from the east on the A625 could join it at Hathersage.

From the centre of Buxton ★ take the A53 signposted to Congleton and, just outside the town (**A**), take the A54 right again to Congleton. At the junction continue straight on towards Macclesfield and, after a few hundred yards, pass the minor road on the right to Derbyshire Bridge where **Walk 8** begins. From the Cat and Fiddle — at 1690 feet the second highest inn in England after Tan Hill in North York-

A stroll through Eyam will reveal some of the fascinating history of this attractive village.

shire — there are grand, sweeping views across the moorland towards the unmistakeable conical outline of Shutlingsloe (1660 feet) and the British Telecom Tower on Sutton Common. In good conditions, the Wrekin and the Welsh hills are also visible. Further on there are also excellent views of the plains of Cheshire and the Manchester conurbation.

On a sharp left-hand bend (**B**), take the minor road on the right to Rainow. Ahead is shapely Kerridge Hill. Turn right on to the A5002 to Whaley Bridge and pass through the village of Rainow, with its attractive stone buildings, some washed pink and some white. The road winds on through some soft, interesting hills before descending into Kettleshulme, a name of probably Scandinavian origin that is rare so far south. At the traffic lights by The White Horse in Whaley Bridge (**C**), turn left towards Stockport (A5004), then after a mile turn left on to the A6, again towards Stockport. After ¼ mile bear right to Chinley on the B6062 (**D**). Off the road to the right in Buxworth, a major restoration scheme is underway at the canal basin — the former terminus of the Peak Forest Canal. This was once a vital artery for moving coal mined in the Peak to the cotton mills of Manchester. Continue through Chinley and then on to the A624 to Chapel-en-le-Frith, passing beneath the spectacular viaducts built at the end of the last century to carry the railway.

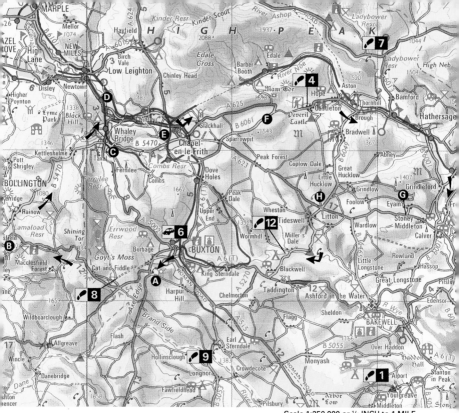

Scale 1:250 000 or ¼ INCH to 1 MILE

Continue straight on at the roundabout by the Ferodo Laboratories (**E**) and turn left towards Buxton at the next junction. After 200 yards bear left, then continue straight on under the A6 towards Rushup and Edale ★. Do not turn right on to the A6! The A625 now climbs back into the Peak District beneath the fine ridge of Rushup Edge — the dividing line between the sombre gritstone scenery of the north and the brilliance of the White Peak to the south. Ahead is the unsightly wound of Eldon Hill Quarry, dubbed 'the best-known eyesore in the Peak'. It was here long before the Park and has provided valuable local employment but public outcry has halted further extension in this otherwise beautiful area of the Peak.

Just past the turning to Edale is a car park where the stroll up Mam Tor ★ commences — it is well worth attaining the summit as there are exceptional views over much of the Peak. Bear right past the turning to the Blue John Cavern — this used to be the A625 to Castleton but landslipping on Mam Tor closed the road below it in 1977 — and then turn left (**F**) down the road signposted Light Traffic Only. This is Winnats Pass ★, one of the most impressive dry gorges in the Peak. Continue straight on at the bottom into Castleton ★ — a good place to stop and explore, and for those feeling like some strenuous

exercise it is also the starting point for **Walk 4**, an upland route giving excellent views.

Continue east out of Castleton on the A625, passing through Hope ★ and Bamford ★, and then into Hathersage ★, turning right opposite The George Hotel on to the B6001 Bakewell road. Follow this along an attractive, wooded section of the Derwent valley into Grindleford ★ and turn right; then after ½ mile turn right again on the B6521 to Eyam ★ where a stroll that will reveal some of the fascinating history of this attractive village is recommended. Follow the road through Eyam to the junction with the A625 (**G**) and turn right towards Stockport. Climb out of Middleton Dale on to the limestone plateau, and look out for Peter's Stone — a rugged limestone knoll — on the left just past the Wardlow turning. Continue to the junction by The Anchor (**H**) and turn left on the B6048 to Tideswell ★, where there is another stroll. Follow the main road through the village and down the attractive, enclosed dale. Just after the road passes under the viaduct carrying the Monsal Trail, there is a turning on the right to the old station where **Walk 12** — which follows the course of the Wye through spectacular Chee Dale — begins. Climb to Blackwell and turn right on to the A6 back to Buxton.

95

TOURS

Tour 7
The Western Moors and the Roaches

39 miles. This tour passes through some remote and peaceful, yet little known, parts of The Peak. On a clear day there are some fine views from the vantage points of Axe Edge, Morridge, and the flanks of The Roaches. Some of the Peak District's finest rock scenery is also to be found en route, too. Not only does it pass the bristling gritstone formations of The Roaches, Hen Cloud, and Ramshaw Rocks, but also one of the Park's most outstanding peaks — Chrome Hill. The tour begins in Buxton but those approaching from Ashbourne and the south could join it near Onecut (G).

Take the A53 Leek Road out of Buxton ★, and stay on it as it climbs on to Axe Edge ★. From here, there are superb views over the White Peak, and noticeable to the left are the jagged crests of Chrome and Parkhouse Hills poking above the surrounding countryside. Turn right off the A53 (A) to Flash ★ and fork right just past the New Inn. As the single track road descends, there are good views of the Dane Valley

ahead. At the junction (B) turn right into Greens, and at the junction after turn left over the bridge to Royal Cottage. Ahead are the craggy outlines of Ramshaw Rocks ★ (left) and The Roaches ★ (right). Soon the road turns sharp left and, at the junction immediately afterwards, follow the road around to the right (C).

You are now crossing Goldsitch Moss, an area where the Lower Coal Measures reach the surface and which were once mined by local people for their low-quality coal. Turn right at the junction by the farms (D) then right again at the next fork, following the road around The Roaches. From the gated road on the western side, there are excellent views over Tittesworth Reservoir, Staffordshire, and the Cheshire Plain. Continue past the turning to Meerbrook and carry straight on underneath the rocky crags of Five Clouds. **Walk 11**, an energetic tour of The Roaches and the wild country to the north, begins here. Pass the isolated bulk of Hen Cloud and continue through Upper Hulme down to the A53. Turn left and continue past Ramshaw Rocks — look out for The Winking Eye Rock on the left! At the next crossroads (E), turn right to Warslow, and after a mile, take the right fork to Leek and Bottomhouses. The airy view over the bristling ridges of The Roaches and Ramshaw Rocks on the right is particularly memo-

Scale 1:250 000 or ¼ INCH to 1 MILE

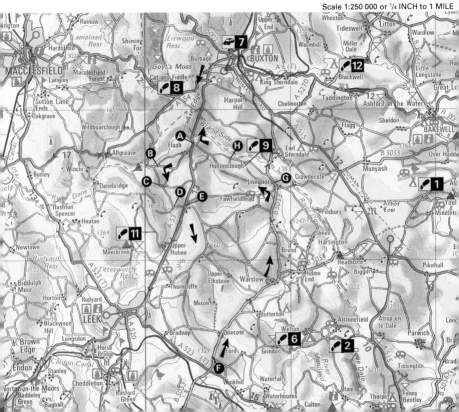

The wild, heather-clad slopes leading up to The Roaches.

rable. Continue past The Mermaid Inn towards Leek and, at the next fork, take the left-hand road signposted 'alternative route'. Bear right immediately afterwards and continue to the B5053 (**F**) along Morridge or 'moor edge'.

Turn left to Onecut and continue through the village and across the pretty valley of Warslow Brook. After Warslow, keep on the B5053, now signposted to Buxton, and note the curving dry stone walls on the right just before entering Longnor ★ , where there is a stroll. Follow the B5053 through Longnor and after about ¼ mile turn left on the road marked Hollinsclough

(**G**). Continue down into the valley and take the right fork to Hollinsclough (**H**). Superb views of the eyecatching peaks of Chrome Hill and Parkhouse Hill now open up on the right, their shapes seeming to change with the different perspective as you proceed along the road. **Walk 9** starts in Hollinsclough and makes a circuit of Chrome Hill. About ½ mile past the village turn left just before the 'Not suitable for motor vehicles' sign down to a junction. Turn right to the A53 then turn right again to Buxton.

Tour 8
The Peak's industrial past

37 miles. This tour incorporates sites of great importance to the industrial archaeologist and is packed with interest — so much so that tourists will have to be selective in what they see if it is to take less than a whole day to complete. The route starts from Matlock, but for those approaching from the west it could start in Bakewell.

Take the A6 south from Matlock ★, through Matlock Bath ★, passing the Peak District Lead Mining Museum and the Temple Mine — both highly recommended for those interested in mining and the geol-ogy of the Peak. Go past the impressive facade of Arkwright's Masson Mill, built in 1784 and still producing textiles today, then turn left (**A**) in Cromford ★ to Lea and go past the ruins of Arkwright's first mill, built in 1771. A stroll around Cromford is recommended and can be started from the canal basin car park on the right just past the mill. Turn right out of the car park, cross the bridge, and bear right, following the river for a mile to the High Peak Junction ★ car park where another interesting stroll begins — this time to the Leawood Pumphouse.

Turn right out of the car park, and pass through Holloway to Crich ★, passing the Tramway Museum. There are fine views from the 950-foot top of the Crich Memorial which can be reached by taking the left

Although Arkwright's Masson Mill is still producing textiles, his first mill is now in ruins.

The magnificent views towards the Kinder Reservoir from Kinder Scout.

'bothy', a term for a basic shepherd's shelter. Turn left on to the A625 in Hope ★ and then right (**C**) on the B6049 to Bradwell ★. The massive chimney belching white smoke belongs to the Hope Valley Cement Works, which has been in existence for over eighty years. Pass through Bradwell, a village with an interesting industrial past. The windsock on the hillside to the left belongs to the Derbyshire and Lancashire Gliding Club, whose superb location offers good ridge soaring. The ridge is being mined underground for feldspar, an important industrial mineral, and the workings are being backfilled to avoid unsightly spoil heaps.

Turn left (**D**) on the road signposted Great Hucklow and, after 100 yards, continue straight on to the tiny village of Foolow ★ which sports an attractive green complete with duckpond, well, and fourteenth-century cross. Leave Foolow for Eyam ★, a village with a fascinating history and famous for the courageous actions of its population who tried to prevent the spread of the plague in 1666. This is a good place to break the journey and take a stroll, which begins at the car park.

Turn left out of the car park, left again down the main street, past the church, then straight on at the junction towards Hathersage ★. A splendid view of Froggatt, Curbar, and Baslow Edges soon unfolds as you descend to the junction with the B6001 where you turn left. In Grindleford ★ carry straight on towards Sheffield on the B6521, passing the turning on the left to Grindleford station where the 3-mile Totley railway tunnel emerges. At the junction with the A625 (**E**), turn left to Hathersage, skirting the interesting rocks of Burbage Moor, and passing Surprise View car park where it might be worth pausing to look at the Derwent Valley and the hills beyond.

Pass through Hathersage where there is an interesting stroll around the village and turn right (**F**) in Bamford ★ on the A6013 to Ladybower. Go through Bamford, past the grassy slopes of the Ladybower Dam, across the bridge to the junction with the A57 and turn left to Glossop. **Walk 7** begins from the lay-by on the left, and a stroll and the energetic **Walk 5** start from Fairholmes ★ Visitor Centre, reached by taking the road on the right immediately after crossing the reservoir. On out-of-season weekdays this can be a particularly tranquil spot to take a break and well worth the extra 7 miles it adds to the tour.

Follow the A57 up the Woodlands Valley where there are impressive views of the northern flanks of Kinder, and climb to the 1630-foot summit of the Snake Pass before descending back into Glossop.

Walking in the Peak District

Winter or summer, rain or shine, these hills are remote and beautiful places which reveal priceless treasures to those who make the effort to wander among them. They do not, however, suffer fools gladly, and anyone tempted to venture into their midst during their wilder moments must be mentally and physically prepared for the conditions they may experience.

The walks described in this book vary in length from 2 to 9 miles and, given good weather, they can be tackled easily by any reasonably fit person. The Peak District is high country by nature, and most walks involve a stiff climb or descent somewhere along the way. Some may present special difficulties under certain conditions and warnings are always given in the introductory texts.

Special care must be taken on all routes during the winter months, however, or when mist or generally poor weather shrouds the hills. Such conditions make navigation difficult and walking physically demanding, and only the experienced and properly equipped walker should venture on to the hills then. Even in summer, care must be taken — a three-hour walk may not seem very long but, if it starts to pour with rain while you are on open moorland without adequate waterproof clothing, then the consequences can be serious. Being lost is also a frightening and potentially dangerous situation especially if you do not have a map and compass, or, just as important, the knowledge of how to use them.

These difficulties can usually be avoided by progressively and methodically building up experience and becoming aware of

Below: *Lathkill Dale can be enjoyed on Walk 1; whilst The Roaches* (right) *are crossed on Walk 11.*

your limitations. Start with the shorter walks and learn from the beginning how to use a map and compass properly — being lost usually results from failing to confirm your position at regular intervals. Doing this frequently will mean that, if any error has occurred, your steps can quickly be retraced before a lot of unexpected ground has been covered.

The Ordnance Survey 1:25,000-scale Pathfinder maps are particularly valuable to walkers, especially when crossing enclosed farmland because they show the routes of footpaths relative to field boundaries. Do remember, though, that maps quickly become out of date — hedges are grubbed up, plantations felled, paths and tracks fall into disuse and become overgrown, while others are created for various reasons.

Build up your walking equipment gradually and thoughtfully, beginning with a comfortable pair of boots (not too heavy), or stout shoes, and some warm and waterproof clothing, including a hat and gloves. A small rucksack is useful for carrying clothes and also enough high-energy food and drink for the walk. Take a little extra just in case, because cold and hunger — or lack of fluid and protective clothing on a hot day — are the walker's greatest enemies. Like the maps and compass, these items will become tried and trusted friends as your experience grows, giving you the confidence to tackle more challenging routes and conditions.

Keep a close eye on the weather, especially when venturing on to the moors, and obtain local forecasts whenever possible. A progressively greying sky, with clouds forming on the highest hills and consistently descending, is a precursor of wind and rain — be prepared to turn back, especially if high, open moorland is to be crossed.

If all this makes excursions into the Peakland hills sound a little too much like hard work on what should be a relaxing ramble, remember that, with experience, the skills, judgement, and stamina required for a safe day on the moors eventually become second nature.

Walk 1
Lathkill Dale and Youlgreave

This is the White Peak at its best, with open, rolling limestone scenery and spectacular deep dales cutting into the heart of the rock. The walk follows the 'young' Lathkill, among beautiful ash woodland of a National Nature Reserve, before passing through gentler scenery of water meadows and lazy, trout-filled pools to the village of Alport. From here it ascends delightful Bradford Dale to Youlgreave, before climbing back on to the limestone plateau. Allow 4 hours for this walk, which uses well-marked paths which are rugged in parts and muddy after heavy rain.

The walk begins from **Moor Lane Picnic Site** (SK 194644) about a mile west of Youlgreave ★. Turn left out of the car park and, at the junction, cross the main road and enter the field at the stile. Follow the well-defined 'Limestone Way' through the

fields to Calling Low Farm where it has recently been diverted to the right of the buildings. Continue downhill through the fields from where there are magnificent panoramic views of the White Peak to the north. Note the concrete dew pond on the left which collects rain water for the farm animals — water is scarce on limestone. Both Calling Low and One Ash Grange Farm ahead on the other side of Cales Dale were owned by monasteries in the Middle Ages and used for the production of wool. As you descend the hillside, the great craggy gashes of Lathkill and Cales dales unfold on the right. Enter the National Nature Reserve and descend the steps.

At the bottom of Cales Dale (**A**), take the path to the right. In wet weather you will see a stream emerging from the limestone below the path but, during dry periods, the upper parts of the Lathkill, in common with many rivers crossing the limestone, will run underground. Cross the footbridge (**B**) and turn right down Lathkill Dale ★. This is the Lathkill at its most spectacular, with limestone crags standing proud high above the river. Notice that the river is full of plant life, in stark contrast to

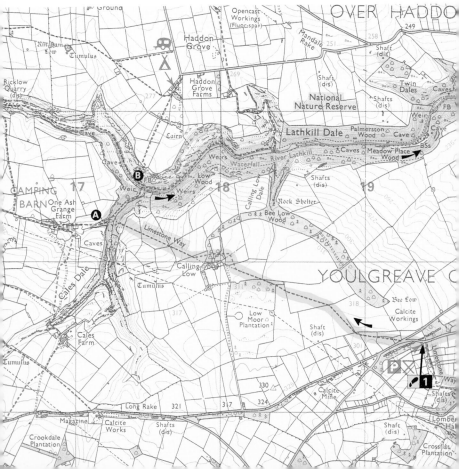

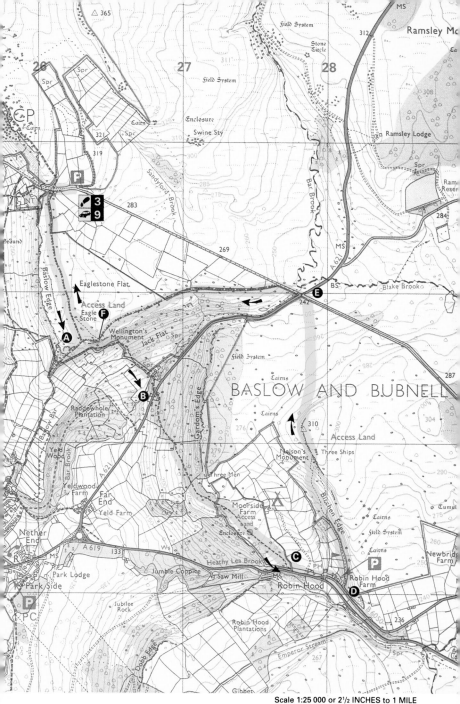

Scale 1:25 000 or 2½ INCHES to 1 MILE

from the Severn Trent Water Authority in 1984 by the Peak Park Planning Board. While it is being made more accessible to the public — its closeness to Chesterfield and Sheffield make it very popular with walkers and day trippers — it is also being managed to conserve and to improve it as a valuable wildlife habitat.

Cross the stile (**E**) and turn left on to the road. Go straight on at the cross roads then, after 200 yards, enter the Access Land through a gate on the left. Follow the course of the old Chesterfield to Baslow road, passing the old inscribed stone marker, to Wellington's Monument, erected in 1816. Bear right here (**F**), then right again at the Eagle Stone, and retrace the route back to the car.

111

Walk 4
Castleton and Mam Tor

Castleton is probably the most popular tourist centre in the Peak, and the Hope Valley area as a whole has more than two million visitors in a year. It is, therefore, rather surprising to find that it is also one of the most densely populated and industrialised parts of the Park, surrounded by quarries and a prominent cement works. But the visitor comes to see the natural wonders that lie close to the northernmost extremity of the White Peak — the many caverns, the spectacular gorges of Cave Dale and Winnats Pass, the shapely summit of Mam Tor, and the impressive artificial structure of Peveril Castle. Our walk is a circuit of the high land around Castleton, and passes close to all these famous features. The views, especially of Kinder Scout from the 1700-foot summit of Mam Tor, are memorable, as is the peaceful climb up the rugged gorge of Cave Dale. Allow 3 hours.

Leave the car in **Castleton ★** village car park and turn left on to the main street, then right to Peveril Castle, passing the Tourist Information Centre. Bear around to the left, past the cross, then take the track on the right to Cave Dale. This is the end of The Limestone Way (**A**), a long-distance path passing through the heart of the White Peak from Matlock ★. Lying on the very edge of Castleton, Cave Dale seems to be overlooked by most casual visitors, and is a great place to escape the bustle of the village below. It is an attractive, dry dale with Peveril Castle standing

guard on its western flank. As you climb the dale you may notice an outcrop of rock, weathered brown; this is 'Derbyshire Toadstone', which is actually a lava extruded from volcanoes on the sea bed some 300 million years ago. The outcrop meets the path just after the first gate, some way up the dale, and the true green/black nature of the rock can be seen on freshly broken samples which have yielded to geologists' hammers.

The path continues up the dale bottom through gates, and eventually to an open field where it carries on ahead for 100 yards to a post marking its junction with a path coming in from back right. Go straight on here (**B**), bearing away from the wall on the right and passing close to the old railway trucks to the corner of the field, and then crossing the stiles to the track. Turn right (**C**) and follow the track to the fork and bear right. After almost a mile, cross the road and the stile, taking the path ahead which eventually crosses the A625 and heads on up the hill. As you converge on the road (**D**), take the obvious path on the right up Mam Tor ★. The pounding of thousands of feet has caused serious erosion problems on the hill which has required the land owner, the National Trust, to close off some of the paths and give this one solid foundations of local stone which can cope with the pressure.

From the summit there are superb views across Edale ★ to the massive bulk of Kinder Scout ★ — the blunt beginning of the wild, dark, gritstone moors of the north. To the south are the emerald-green upland pastures of the White Peak, sadly disfigured by the many quarries that sink like huge ulcers into the flesh of the land. Mam Tor lies on a ridge of shales and grits

Mam Tor.

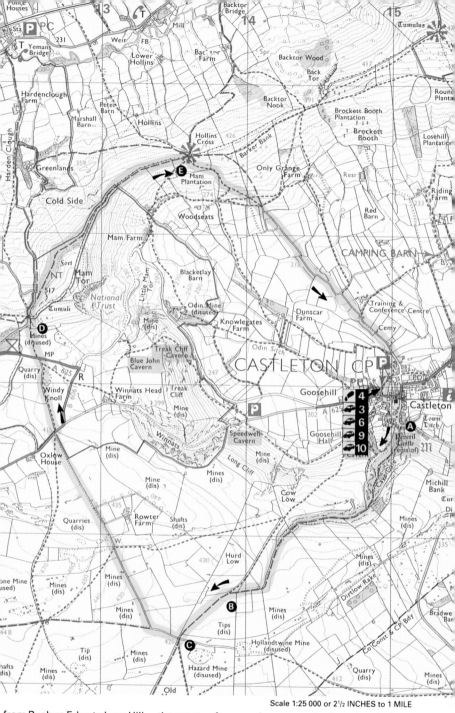

from Rushup Edge to Lose Hill — the great divide between these two contrasting landscapes. The shales are unstable, and give the hill its local name of 'Shivering Mountain'. Its eastern face is subject to landslides, troublesome enough to have caused the permanent closure of part of the A625 in 1977 — the remains of which can still be seen below. The steep eastern face can be approached cautiously from the summit.

From the summit follow the ridge-top path to Hollins Cross (**E**) and turn right downhill, eventually turning right again at the sign to Backtor and Lose Hill. Follow the road back towards Castleton and take the path on the right by Millbridge House back to the car park.

Walk 5
Alport Castles and the Derwent Reservoirs

This is a tough walk with a short section of high, desolate moorland and should not be attempted by inexperienced hillwalkers in poor weather. A compass should be carried. For the fit, properly equipped and provisioned walker, however, the rewards are great, as the route passes the rugged cliffs and pinnacles of Alport Castles. These were one of the original Seven Wonders of the Peak, and a few centuries ago they were home to golden eagles. Allow at least 5 hours and be prepared to turn back should the moor above the Castles be shrouded in mist.

The walk begins from the **Fairholmes ★** Car Park and Picnic Site (SK 173893), situated 2 miles down a minor road which leaves the A57 at the western end of the Ladybower Viaduct. Leave the car park by the normal vehicle exit and take the concessionary footpath opposite the road junction. At the marker post, take the footpath straight on to Lockerbrook. Cross the concrete water course and again take the path to Lockerbrook. When you meet the forest walk trail turn left and, at the junction to Lockerbrook Farm, bear right and continue up the hill, keeping to the yellow marker posts. Leave the plantation by the stile and carry on up the field to a track.

Turn left (**A**) and follow the track past the farm to a complicated junction of tracks (**B**). Take the one that bears around to the right. From here there are good views of the eastern end of Kinder Scout ★, Lose Hill and even the Hope Valley Cement Works! Lose Hill is also known as Ward's Piece, named after the great pioneering rambler J.H.B.Ward, who founded the Sheffield Clarion Ramblers Club in 1900,

The award-winning car park and picnic site at Fairholmes.

and later went on to become the first chairman of the National Standing Council of Ramblers Associations, now known simply as the Ramblers Association. The Sheffield ramblers bought 54 acres on the summit of Lose Hill and gave it to J.H.B.Ward in 1945 in appreciation of his work for the rambling movement, and he in turn gave the land to the National Trust.

Follow the track down past Rowlee Farm, cross the A57, and take the road opposite down to the river. Exposures of the soft shales that underlie the Millstone Grit of surrounding hills can be seen where the River Ashop has cut through them. Cross the river (**C**) and continue along the tarmac track to within 100 yards of Upper Ashop farm then bear right on to the bridleway,

With conical hills behind, the river bubbles down through Alport Dale.

The Derwent Dam, holding back the Derwent Reservoir.

eventually crossing the river by a footbridge. Recross the A57 (**D**) and take the path opposite, which runs close to the river at first then crosses a field and meets a track. Turn right and follow the track to Alport Farm, passing through the buildings and bearing around to the right after the second house to follow the path down to the river.

Cross the footbridge (**E**), turn left, then right uphill at the sign. Keep close to the fence around the new plantation on the right — the path becomes more distinct as it climbs. Views of the impressive structure of the Tower begin to unfold. It was once attached to the plateau above, but the river cut into the old rocks below it and eventually a large mass of rock began to crumble and slip slowly downhill, the Tower remaining relatively intact. Join a wall on the right, then cross a stile and walk to the right of the same wall as it continues around the Castles. Once on the plateau, follow the cliffs. From here there are captivating views of Alport Dale and an impression of the vastness of the Pennine Plateau can be gained. Below, the rugged splendour of rocks and stones and the vastness of the gritstone cliffs leave no doubt that if humanity permits, the golden eagles will one day return — just as they are now returning to the Lake District.

Follow the cliffs as far as a tumble-down dry stone wall (**F**), then turn right and follow it down hill. Notice how the peat has eroded into hags dissected by groughs — this is typical of the acid Pennine moorlands. Where the wall ends, bear slightly left and follow the vehicle track down hill. Either side are grouse butts — hides used by shooting parties when the moor is closed to walkers for a few days each year. Enter the plantation through a gate and follow the track to a junction and turn right. At the road (**G**), turn right and follow it to the start of the path on the left just past the second dam continuing on through woodland back to the car park.

Walk 6
Thor's Cave and the Manifold Valley

Like the neighbouring Dove, the lower Manifold has cut a dramatic valley through limestone country although, unlike the Dove, a long stretch of its bed may be dry during the summer months as it flows through a system of underground caverns from Wettonmill to Ilam. Our walk starts in the quiet village of Wetton before visiting the magnificent natural cavern of Thor's Cave, then descending through woodland to the Manifold. From here we ascend through woods and fields to the scattered village of Grindon before descending once again via a tributary stream through peaceful fields and meadows to the Manifold at Wettonmill. The route returns to Wetton along a remote, treeless valley, and between bare hills of limestone. Allow 4 hours for this energetic walk and expect some slippery slopes especially after rain.

Turn right out of the car park in **Wetton** (SK 109552), then right again down the lane towards Wetton Mill. Turn left at the next junction (**A**) and, after 50 yards, turn left on to the waymarked concessionary path to Thor's Cave. The promontory containing Thor's Cave is formed from reef limestone and can be seen ahead; beyond it there is the village of Grindon with its distinctive church spire. Leave the track and cross the stile, then follow the waymarked path close to the wall on the left at first and cross the fields to the cave. Take care as the paths close to the cave are steep and slippery when wet!

The cave has been disfigured somewhat by climbers' hardware hanging from its roof but is none the less impressive. Deposits in the cave have revealed remains of bear, hyena, sabre-toothed tiger, and also humans, who occupied it in more recent times. The west 'window' leads to nothing so return to the entrance and descend the steps, taking the left fork where the path splits to the valley bottom. Cross

The Manifold Valley.

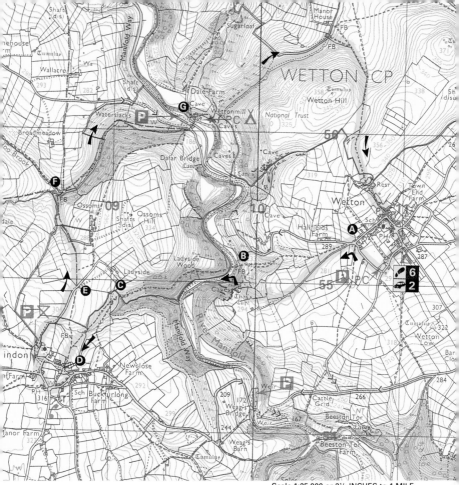

Scale 1:25 000 or 2½ INCHES to 1 MILE

the footbridge (**B**) over the Manifold ★ (the river bed may be dry during the summer months) and go over the stile ahead. Continue across the Manifold track and cross the stile into Ladyside Wood. Follow the path uphill and around to the left at the junction, then follow the waymark up some steps — it is worth glancing back for an impressive view of Thor's Cave.

The path continues along the hillside, eventually leaving the wood. Cross the stile by the big stone trough (**C**), and slant left uphill, eventually walking parallel to the stream. Cross the stone stile in the hedge/wall near the corner of the field, then go over the stream at the footbridge. Head to the left of the church and follow the markers to the road. At the road (**D**), turn left; then, after 50 yards, take the right fork. Turn right at the junction and walk along the road past the pub, bearing around to the right at the next junction. After another 50 yards take the No Through Road on the left. The scenery is now rather gentler than the land crossed to the east of the Manifold Valley, with hedges rather than dry stone walls — features character-

istic of the underlying shales and shale grits.

After ½ mile cross an unmarked stile next to a gate on the left (**E**). Head across the field, then climb over the stile. Make your way down to the right of the old hedge line to a stile in the fence, cross this and continue to another stile, then ahead to the left of the trees before picking up a faint path down to the footbridge. Cross the footbridge (**F**) and continue to the gate ahead, across another footbridge, and follow the path close to the river to Wettonmill. At Wettonmill (**G**) cross the Manifold, then turn right and go past the tea rooms (a welcome spot to take a rest perhaps), taking a path up some steps between the buildings in the corner of the yard. Go through the gate and climb the ridge ahead, then turn left towards a gate in some trees, and follow the path down to the stream. Ascend this delightful, secluded valley, and turn right down the steps opposite the Manor House. Follow the dry stone wall on the right up the hill. Cross the next two fields and follow a well-defined path back into Wetton.

Walk 7
The Ladybower Reservoir and Derwent Moor

This interesting and fairly easy walk follows the well-made bridleway through the woodlands on the eastern side of the reservoir before climbing the wild, open moorland beneath Derwent Edge. It returns via the splendid viewpoint of Lead Hill, before descending back to the Ladybower. Allow 2 hours and expect some mud on the boggy areas of the moorland.

Park in the layby close to the telephone box at the eastern end of the **Ladybower Viaduct** (SK 196874). Cross the road and turn left, taking the bridleway along the private road which bears off to the right. Follow this well-made track alongside the reservoir, passing through woodland and eventually around an inlet. Among the trees by the water's edge can be seen all that remains of Grainfoot Farm which, like

many other farms and houses, was abandoned when the reservoir was filled in 1943. The villages of Ashopton and Derwent were lost beneath the flood, and their occupants rehoused at Yorkshire Bridge, just south of the Ladybower Dam. This structure, now grassed over, is 140 feet high and 1250 feet long, and holds back over 6000 million gallons of water — used to quench the thirst of Derby, Sheffield, Leicester, and Nottingham.

Soon after crossing a stream (Grindle Clough), go through a gate and then turn right on to a footpath (**A**). Follow this diagonally across the field, eventually reaching the corner of a fence, and then bearing left to follow it to the barn. Pass through the gate to the left of the barn, then around the back and through another gate. Carry on and cross the Grindle Clough, following the path to Moscar. Go through a gate and keep to the left of the walls, eventually passing between a wall and plantation before reaching a gate (**B**) to open country. Ahead is Derwent Edge, capped with tors bearing weird, evocative names such as Salt Cellar, Wheel Stones, and Cakes of Bread. To the north lies some truly wild moorland. Dangerous to the ill-

Scale 1:25 000 or 2½ INCHES to 1 MILE

equipped and inexperienced, many lives have been lost on this bleak, windswept wilderness over the years. Two miles to the north 'Lost Lad' marks the spot where, in the sixteenth century, a thirteen-year-old boy from a valley farm tragically became lost on the moor and perished in the cold. His remains were not found until years later and legend has it that he had scratched the words 'lost lad' on a nearby stone.

Bear right across the moor, which may be muddy, and pass through a gap in the long wall ahead. Turn right and keep to the left of the wall, following it for about 100 yards after it finishes (**C**). It is worth climbing the extra few feet up the promontory on the right where there are fine views over the surrounding countryside. Return to the path and descend the gully on the well-defined path, bearing left to follow the wall, and eventually passing through a gate into a plantation. Continue through the plantation and pass through the gate at the end, then turn right along the track back to the road.

Fishing in the tranquillity of the Ladybower Reservoir. It is hard to believe that beneath these waters are two drowned villages.

Walk 8
The Goyt Valley

For the novice hill walker, the Upper Goyt Valley is an excellent area to experience the openness of the Dark Peak. The route is easy to follow and the diverse bird life and interesting geology make it an attractive route for the natural historian. Allow 1½ hours.

The walk starts from the car park and picnic site near **Derbyshire Bridge** (SK 019716) and is best approached by the minor roads from the A537. The road from Errwood Reservoir is one way (uphill traffic only) and may be closed completely on Sundays and bank holidays from 10.30 am to 5.30 pm. It is hard to believe that the Upper Goyt valley once supported a thriving farming community and factories making paints and explosives. These disappeared beneath Fernilee and Errwood Reservoirs, however, constructed in 1938 and 1968 respectively to provide water for Stockport. From the car park follow the track to Berry Clough. Look out for the speckle face Dale O'Goyt sheep — a breed that originated here, and now commonly known as the Derbyshire Gritstone. From this old road there are good views towards Buxton ★. At the top of the rise (**A**), take the path on the left to Berry Clough, marked with a yellow arrow and a number 6. The path is obvious and again marked where it bears left. At the junction of paths (**B**), carry on down hill.

The moor is the haunt of grouse — large, dark-brown birds which 'explode' from the cover of the heather and fly off with rapid whirring wing beats interspersed with short glides. The males are darker than the females and have red crests. Their call is an unmistakeable, loud 'go back, go back'. Grouse feed mainly on young shoots of heather and the moors are periodically burnt to encourage new growth. The shooting season begins on 12 August — 'The Glorious Twelfth' — and upland areas of the Park subject to access agreements may be closed to walkers for a few days while shooting takes place. Curlew, meadow pipits, golden plover, and twite also live on the moorlands, while birds such as the ring ouzel, (smaller than a blackbird and with a white throat), linnets, and whinchats prefer the deep-sided cloughs. In fact, the diversity of bird life has led the Nature Conservancy Council to designate the area a Site of Special Scientific Interest (SSSI). The moor is not entirely clad with heather for there are areas of bracken and, in the wetter parts, cotton-grass.

Continue descending to the right of the small stream, crossing the footbridge at the bottom and climbing to the road (**C**). Turn left and walk along the road passing through a very attractive valley, with deep cloughs cutting through the shales to the Goyt. Look closely at the dark, shaly exposures close to Derbyshire Bridge. There are, in fact, thin bands of very low-grade coal among these — dark grey and difficult for the untrained eye to detect. These seams were, however, mined on a commercial scale during the last century, mainly using bell pits, where vertical shafts were sunk into the seam and coal extracted radially from the base to give the characteristic bell-shaped cavern. Much of the coal was burnt with limestone to produce quicklime. The workings extend from Derbyshire bridge to Burbage.

Follow the road all the way back to the car park.

Errwood Reservoir, one of two providing water for Stockport.

Goyt's Moss

Goytsclough
Quarry

C

Deep
Clough

Stake Clough

73

Goyt's Clough

Berry Clough

B

Ravens
Low

Waterfall

Foxhole Hollow

Jacob's
Cabin

436

Raven's
Low Flat

479

MS

A

72

Fiddle

Derbyshire
Bridge

P ✕ PC

HARTINGTON UPPER QUARTER CP

499

8
4
6

MP

Scale 1:25 000 or 2½ INCHES to 1 MILE

123

Walk 9
Chrome Hill and the Upper Dove Valley

Chrome Hill may only just top 1400 feet but it is probably the National Park's only real claim to a true 'Peak' in the rugged, mountain sense. Strange to think that 300 million years ago, it was a reef in a shallow sea! Allow 2 hours for this walk among outstanding and unspoilt scenery.

Park on the roadside near the telephone box in **Hollinsclough** (SK 065664), 2 miles north-west of Longnor ★ . Go through the village on the same road, heading up the hill. About 100 yards past the last building on the right, pass through a gate in the fence (**A**) and follow the bridlepath downhill to the left of the wall. Where the wall ends, bear right down to the footbridge over the infant Dove ★ . Cross the bridge, go through the gate, then bear left up to the corner of the field. Turn left on to the track (**B**), and follow it past the farm at Fough and eventually Booth Farm. Where the track forks bear right (**C**) towards Stoop Farm. The track passes through a tumbledown wall, then after another hundred yards bears right. Leave it here and take the faint path across the fields and, close to the shelter belt behind the farm, bear off left towards a gateway. A new concessionary path across the ridge of Chrome Hill starts from here, which may prove irresistible to the serious hill walker! Your route follows the track to the road (**D**), however, then turns right.

Continue past Greensides and eventually descend beautiful Dowel Dale. On the right is Dowel Cave, where remains of Stone Age people and domesticated animals have been found buried among an accumulation of silts, clays, and gravels. Opposite Dowel Hall a spring gushes forth where the limestone meets impermeable shale, and the resulting stream follows the road where a dramatic scene of breathtaking beauty begins to unfold. Ahead are the rugged peaks of Chrome Hill at 1417 feet, and Parkhouse Hill at 1221 feet (both famous for their fossils), enclosing a natural, grassy floored amphitheatre. Follow the road between the peaks, then turn sharp right (**E**) on to the track between the stone gateposts. Where the track turns sharp left to the farmhouse carry straight on along the dirt track. You may have noticed that hedges have largely replaced dry stone walls in the upper Dove valley where the underlying rocks are shales and shale grits. Exposures of these rocks can be seen in the bed of the Swallow Brook. Notice, too, how the ground turns black as the track cuts through a seam of low-quality coal.

Cross the footbridge and follow the track to a junction (**F**), then turn left to the road, turning right back to Hollinsclough.

A distant view of the Chrome and Packhouse hills.

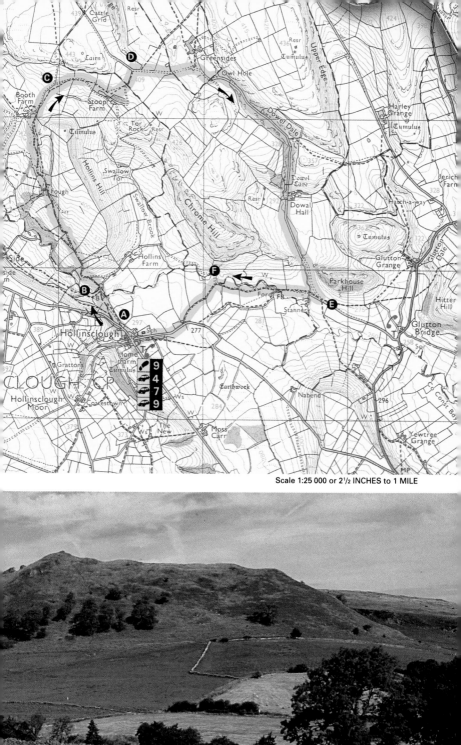

Scale 1:25 000 or 2½ INCHES to 1 MILE

Walk 10
Stanton Moor

Stanton Moor is an isolated island of mill-stone grit in a sea of softer rocks. In a sense, its summit plateau supports a lost world, for the concentration of Bronze Age remains is particularly dense. Its stone circles and tumuli may give it a strong air of mystery. It is not a dark, sombre place, however, but rather has the light, airy feel of a lowland heath. From its edges there are fine views of the surrounding countryside. Allow 1½ hours for the walk which is easy to follow.

Park the car opposite the quarry just northeast of **Birchover ★** (SK 241625) on the Stanton-in-Peak road. The quarry is still worked for its Millstone Grit. Turn left out of the car park, heading for Stanton-in-Peak. After 400 yards turn right (**A**) between the posts, on to the track blocked to cars by a large rock. Cross the stile and continue to the Cork Stone. This strange monolith had iron rungs set into it in Victorian times, no doubt to aid ascent. The

steps enlarged by the thousands of feet that have scaled it are clearly visible — if you are tempted, then remember that getting back down is the hard part! Continue past the Cork Stone to a junction of paths (**B**) and turn left. On the right are the remains of a burial mound, of which there are at least seventy on the moor, dating from the Early Bronze Age (2000-1400 BC). Earlier this century, the Heathcote family of Birchover excavated many of these and their finds, which include cremation remains, flints, and polished jet, are now to be found in the City Museum, Sheffield.

As you continue northwards, you will see a large stone circle off to the left before the birch wood and, soon after, the Nine Ladies Stone Circle can be found among the woods, again on the left. This may once have contained a burial mound and had considerable significance. Like some other similar sites in Britain, a pointer stone (King Stone) stands alone some distance from the circle. The site was surrounded by a protective wall, but thankfully this was removed in 1985. About 50 yards past the Nine Ladies Stone Circle (**C**) turn right to a stile. Cross this and follow the path around to the right. The Reform

Scale 1:25 000 or 2½ INCHES to 1 MILE

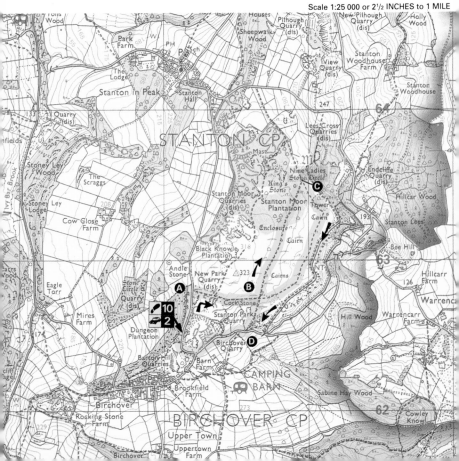

The Cork Stone, with its footholds enlarged by the thousands of feet that have scaled it.

Tower was built by the Thornhills in 1832 in tribute to Lord Grey and his Reform Bill. The 28 acres of land on which it stands now belong to the National Trust. From the edge there are good views over Darley Dale ★ and the attractive village of Winster ★ .

Continue to the left of the fence, past the Cat Stone to the road. Turn right (**D**) and at the junction right again back to the car park.

Walk 11
Lud's Church and
The Roaches

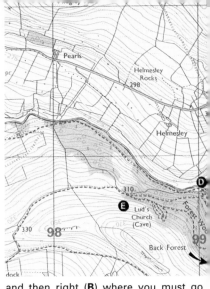

This strenuous walk passes through some remote and fascinating gritstone country, full of myth and mystery. It begins at the southern tip of The Roaches, then winds north along lonely paths and roads across Goldsitch Moss, around Gradbach Hill overlooking the beautiful wooded valley of the Black Brook. From Gradbach it climbs through attractive woodland to the awesome chasm of Lud's Church before following the ridge and returning across the spectacular ridge of The Roaches. Allow 4 hours for the main walk, and 1¹/₂ hours for the alternative, gentler circuit of The Roaches.

Park in the lay-by at the southern end of **The Roaches** ★ (SK 004621), about 1 mile north-west of Upper Hulme — best reached by leaving the A53 at one of the Upper Hulme turnings and following the road through the village. Go through the gate at the end and follow the track up hill to the right, between Hen Cloud and The Roaches, passing through a gap in the wall and then following the wall on the right. The path eventually bears away from the wall, crosses a stream, then carries straight on becoming more distinct. Cross the stile (**A**) and turn left, following the track straight on to the road. Turn right, then left at the next two road junctions. The road is straight for a mile, as it crosses desolate Goldsitch Moss. You are now in the centre of the Goyt syncline, a fold in the rocks which runs from just north of Buxton ★, south to Leek.

The rocks visible as The Roaches slope into the ground, turn beneath your feet and rise again to become Ramshaw Rocks ★. The youngest rocks — in this case the lower Coal Measures — lie just beneath the surface at this point, and were once extensively mined, probably by farmers subsidising what meagre income they could eke out of this poor land. All that remains of their toil are the small spoil heaps that dot the boggy moor. These same Coal Measures are also crossed on **Walks 8** and **9**. In each location the seams are very thin and the coal of poor quality — very different from the later, richer Coal Measures found on either side of the Peak District. The coal mined on Goldsitch probably went to fire the many lime kilns in the area.

The road will eventually turn sharp left and then right (**B**) where you must go straight on, following the footpath to Gradbach. Cross the stile and keep to the right of the wall, eventually passing through a gap and then keeping to the left of the wall ahead. The path now passes through two more tumbledown walls before converging on the wall on the left. Follow it to the end of the next field, then go left for a few yards and again follow the wall on the left, eventually passing between walls and then continuing through the farmyard ahead. Follow the track to the road. Turn left (**C**) into the YHA grounds, and go around the back of the hostel. This impressive building was once a silk mill, built in 1758 and driven by a large waterwheel powered by the River Dane. Pass through a gate, then climb the steps and cross the stile. Follow the path close to the river as far as a footbridge.

Cross the bridge (**D**) and go straight on to Swythamley, turning right after 50 yards on to a well-made path. On reaching the rocks (**E**) — from where there are inviting views along the Dane Valley — turn back left to Lud's Church and, after 200 yards, take a well-defined path on the right through the chasm. This spectacular cleft in the rocks is the result of a huge landslip. Part of the hillside has broken away and slipped a few feet down hill, revealing a crack about 15 feet wide and 50 feet deep in places. This strange place is thought to be The Green Chapel sought by Sir Gawain, in the famous medieval poem *Sir Gawain and the Green Knight*. A hunting lodge at nearby Swythamley may well have been the Green Knight's Castle. As you leave from the other end, follow the concessionary footpath to a junction with another path then turn right, following it through the fringes of this beautiful wood.

At the sign post (**F**) turn right to Roach End. Climb the hill, keeping to the right of

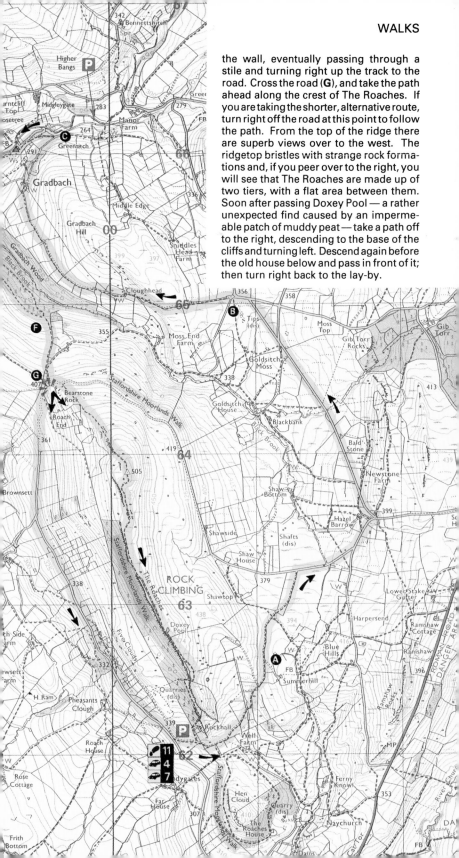

the wall, eventually passing through a stile and turning right up the track to the road. Cross the road (**G**), and take the path ahead along the crest of The Roaches. If you are taking the shorter, alternative route, turn right off the road at this point to follow the path. From the top of the ridge there are superb views over to the west. The ridgetop bristles with strange rock formations and, if you peer over to the right, you will see that The Roaches are made up of two tiers, with a flat area between them. Soon after passing Doxey Pool — a rather unexpected find caused by an impermeable patch of muddy peat — take a path off to the right, descending to the base of the cliffs and turning left. Descend again before the old house below and pass in front of it; then turn right back to the lay-by.

Walk 12
Chee Dale and the Monsal Trail

The drama of water and rock in Chee Dale is unrivalled elsewhere in the Peak and, now that the trains have gone, these remote splendours are accessible only to trail users. This is not a walk for the nervous or infirm, however, because there are steep, slippery descents and a difficult section beneath overhanging cliffs along the riverbed — this may be impassable in very wet weather. Footpath erosion is also becoming a problem and, for these reasons, the route is best reserved for dry periods. Allow at least 2½ hours.

Start from the car park at the old railway station in **Miller's Dale** (SK 138733), 5½ miles east of Buxton ★. When approaching from Buxton take the A6 towards Bakewell ★ and, near Blackwell, turn left on to the B6049 towards Tideswell ★. Take the minor road on the left to the car park immediately after crossing the Wye.

Tours 1 and **6** also follow the B6049 and pass close to the start of the walk. From the old station, head west along the course of the railway. On the right are the East Buxton Lime Kilns, built in the 1880s to supply the increasing demands of the iron and steel industries. The kilns were originally cut straight into the rock, the concrete reinforcing buttresses being added during the 1920s. Coal was brought in by train and used to bake local limestone at high temperature to produce quicklime (calcium oxide) which was then shipped out by train.

The Chee Tor Tunnel ahead is closed, so leave the trail and take the path off to the right (**A**) to Chee Dale. The path descends steeply to the river and there are good views of the viaduct. At the bottom, turn right and follow the riverside path. Cross the footbridge (**B**) and climb the hillside ahead just to the left of the crag. Pass through a gap in a tumbledown wall and bear right. Climb to the top of the field and pass through a gap in the wall and continue straight on, converging with the field boundary on the left and eventually coming to a stile. Note the exposure of 'Toadstone' — a volcanic rock that solidified on

Scale 1:25 000 or 2½ INCHES to 1 MILE

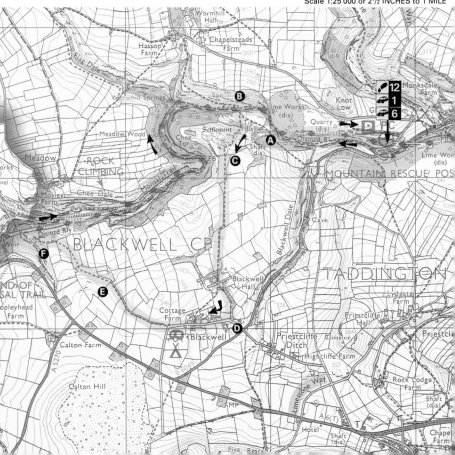

A view of the viaduct at Monsal Head.

the sea-floor some 300 million years ago. The views of Chee Dale from here already hint at its spectacular nature, soon to be revealed.

Cross the stile (**C**) and continue ahead, keeping close to the wall on the right, and turning right between walls in the corner of the field. Cross the stile and bear left, following the track to the right of the wall to the farm. Pass through the farm buildings and bear left down the farm drive. At the road (**D**) bear right and, at the sharp left bend, go straight on across the stile and follow the track between the walls. Where the track ends (**E**) follow the wall on the right at first then continue straight on, crossing the stile to the left of the ruined house. Head for the stile in the far left-hand corner of this next field, cross it, and follow the wall on the right; then cross another stile into open land above the gorge. Follow the wall on the left at first, then continue straight on down a path,

descending steeply to a stile below left.

Cross the stile in the dale bottom (**F**) and turn right. Soon, cross the stile to the left of the bridge and turn right on to the Monsal Trail. Follow the trail through two tunnels and, before the blocked entrance to Chee Tor Tunnel, take the concessionary path off to the right, and cross the footbridge to the far bank. The really interesting bit now begins: follow the stepping stones along the river bed below the cliff! If the stones are submerged — which may happen after heavy rain — then be prepared to turn back. The gorge here is truly wild and spectacular — well worth the effort spent getting here.

Follow the Wye past Wormhill Springs, where water gushes from holes in the ground during wet weather, and walk around to the footbridge crossed earlier. Retrace the route back to the station.

131

CONVENTIONAL SIGNS   1:250 000 or 1 INCH to 4 MILES

ROADS
Not necessarily rights of way

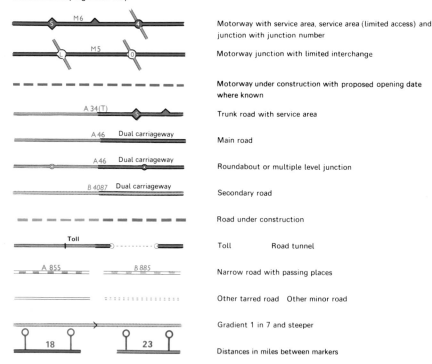

Motorway with service area, service area (limited access) and junction with junction number

Motorway junction with limited interchange

Motorway under construction with proposed opening date where known

Trunk road with service area

Main road

Roundabout or multiple level junction

Secondary road

Road under construction

Toll   Road tunnel

Narrow road with passing places

Other tarred road   Other minor road

Gradient 1 in 7 and steeper

Distances in miles between markers

The representation of a road is no evidence of the existence of a right of way

PRIMARY ROUTES

These form a national network of recommended through routes which complement the motorway system. Selected places of major traffic importance are known as Primary Route Destinations and are shown thus **BUXTON** Distances and directions to such destinations are repeated on traffic signs which, on primary routes, have a green background or, on motorways, have a blue background.
To continue on a primary route through or past a place which has appeared as a destination on previous signs, follow the directions to the next primary destination shown on the green-backed signs.

RAILWAYS

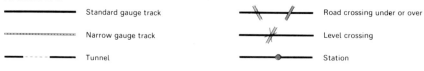

Standard gauge track

Narrow gauge track

Tunnel

Road crossing under or over

Level crossing

Station

WATER FEATURES

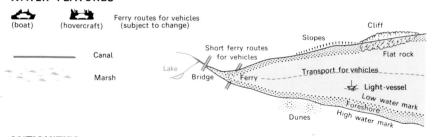

(boat)   (hovercraft)   Ferry routes for vehicles (subject to change)

Canal

Marsh

Lake

Bridge   Ferry

Short ferry routes for vehicles

Cliff

Slopes

Flat rock

Transport for vehicles

Light-vessel

Low water mark
Foreshore
High water mark

Dunes

ANTIQUITIES

※ Native fortress   ✕ Site of battle (with date)   - - - - - Roman road (course of)   CANOVIUM ▪ Roman antiquity

𝕮astle ▪   Other antiquities

𝔪   Ancient Monuments and Historic Buildings in the care of the Secretaries of State for the Environment, for Scotland and for Wales and that are open to the public.

BOUNDARIES

+ — + — + — + — National

— — — — — — — { County, Region or Islands Area

GENERAL FEATURES

 Buildings

 Wood

 Lighthouse (in use)   Lighthouse (disused)

Windmill   Radio or TV mast

▲ Youth hostel

⊕ { with Customs facilities
✈ } Civil aerodrome { without Customs facilities

Ⓗ Heliport

☎ Public telephone

☎ Motoring organisation telephone

┼ Intersection, latitude & longitude at 30' intervals (not shown where it confuses important detail)

TOURIST INFORMATION

✝ Abbey, Cathedral, Priory

🐟 Aquarium

⛺ Camp site

🚐 Caravan site

🏰 Castle

Cave

Ⓨ Windmill
Ⓨ Country park

✧ Craft centre

❀ Garden

▶ Golf course or links

🏛 Historic house

ℹ Information centre

Motor racing

🖼 Museum

! Nature or forest trail

🦆 Nature reserve

☆ Other tourist feature

✕ Picnic site

🚂 Preserved railway

🏇 Racecourse

⛷ Skiing

🔭 Viewpoint

🦌 Wildlife park

🐘 Zoo

WALKS, CYCLE & MOTOR TOURS
Applicable to all scales

 Start point of walk

➡ Route of walk

Featured walk

 Start point of tour

➡ Route of tour

Featured tour

 Start point of mini-walk

Featured mini-walk

FOLLOW THE COUNTRY CODE
Enjoy the countryside and respect its life and work

Guard against all risk of fire

Fasten all gates

Keep your dogs under close control

Keep to public paths across farmland

Leave livestock, crops and machinery alone

Use gates and stiles to cross fences, hedges and walls

Take your litter home

Help to keep all water clean

Protect wildlife, plants and trees

Take special care on country roads

Make no unnecessary noise

CONVENTIONAL SIGNS
1:25 000 or 2½ INCHES to 1 MILE

ROADS AND PATHS

Not necessarily rights of way

M I or A 6(M)	M I or A 6(M)	Motorway
A 31 (T)	A 31(T)	Trunk road
A 35	A 35	Main road
B 3074	B 3074	Secondary road
A 35	A 35	Dual carriageway

Narrow roads with passing places are annotated

Road generally more than 4m wide

Road generally less than 4m wide

Other road, drive or track

Unfenced roads and tracks are shown by pecked lines

.... Path

RAILWAYS

—————	Multiple track ⎤ Standard
—•—•—•—	Single track ⎦ gauge
——+——+——	Narrow gauge
———|—	Siding
Cutting	
Embankment	
—•——•—	Tunnel
Road over & under	
Level crossing; station	

PUBLIC RIGHTS OF WAY

Public rights of way may not be evident on the ground

- - - - - - - - ⎤ } Public paths { Footpath
— — — — ⎦ Bridleway

+ + + + + Byway open to all traffic
—•—•—•— Road used as a public path

The indication of a towpath in this book does not necessarily imply a public right of way
The representation of any other road, track or path is no evidence of the existence of a right of way

DANGER AREA

MOD ranges in the area
Danger!
Observe warning notices

⊕ Mountain Rescue Post

BOUNDARIES

— · — · — County (England and Wales)

— — — — District

—∘—∘—∘— London Borough

· · · · · · · Civil Parish (England)* Community (Wales)

— — — — — Constituency (County, Borough, Burgh or European Assembly)

⎱ Coincident boundaries are shown by the first appropriate symbol

*For Ordnance Survey purposes County Boundary is deemed to be the limit of the parish structure whether or not a parish area adjoins

SYMBOLS

♟	Church	with tower
♦	or	with spire
+	chapel	without tower or spire

▣ △		Glasshouse; youth hostel
⬭		Bus or coach station
☼ ⚓ ⏚		Lighthouse; lightship; beacon
△		Triangulation station

♦ ♦	} Triangulation point on {	church or chapel
⏚		lighthouse, beacon
▱ ⊙		building; chimney

Electricity
pylon pole transmission line

VILLA	Roman antiquity (AD 43 to AD 420)
Castle	Other antiquities
⚔	Site of antiquity
⚔ 1066	Site of battle (with date)
	Gravel pit
	Sand pit
	Chalk pit, clay pit or quarry
	Refuse or slag heap
▨▨▨▨	Sloping wall

▢	Water	▢	Mud
▢	Sand; sand & shingle		
▨	National Park or Forest Park Boundary		
NT	National Trust always open		
NT	National Trust opening restricted		
FC	Forestry Commission		

VEGETATION
Limits of vegetation are defined by positioning of the symbols but may be delineated also by pecks or dots

Coniferous trees	Scrub	Reeds
Non-coniferous trees	Bracken, rough grassland	Marsh
Coppice	In some areas bracken (α) and rough grassland (····) are shown separately	Shown collectively as rough grassland on some sheets
Orchard	Heath	Saltings

HEIGHTS AND ROCK FEATURES

Vertical face

50 · ⎤ Determined ⎱ ground survey
285 · ⎦ by ⎰ air survey

Surface heights are to the nearest metre above mean sea level. Heights shown close to a triangulation pillar refer to the station height at ground level and not necessarily to the summit

Loose rock   Boulders   Outcrop   Scree

Contours are at 5 metres vertical interval

ABBREVIATIONS
1:25 000 or 2½ INCHES to 1 MILE also 1:10 000/1:10 560 or 6 INCHES to 1 MILE

BP,BS	Boundary Post or Stone	P	Post Office	A,R	Telephone, AA or RAC
CH	Club House	Pol Sta	Police Station	TH	Town Hall
F V	Ferry Foot or Vehicle	PC	Public Convenience	Twr	Tower
FB	Foot Bridge	PH	Public House	W	Well
HO	House	Sch	School	Wd Pp	Wind Pump
MP,MS	Mile Post or Stone	Spr	Spring		
Mon	Monument	T	Telephone, public		

Abbreviations applicable only to 1:10 000/1:10 560 or 6 INCHES to 1 MILE

Ch	Church	GP	Guide Post	TCB	Telephone Call Box
F Sta	Fire Station	P	Pole or Post	TCP	Telephone Call Post
Fn	Fountain	S	Stone	Y	Youth Hostel

Maps and Mapping

Most early maps of the area covered by this guide were published on a county basis, and, if you wish to follow their development in detail, R. V. Tooley's *Maps and Map Makers* will be found most useful. The first significant county maps were produced by Christopher Saxton in the 1570s, the whole of England and Wales being covered in only six years. Although he did not cover the whole country, John Norden, working at the end of the sixteenth century, was the first map-maker to show roads. In 1611-12, John Speed, making use of Saxton's and Norden's pioneer work, produced his *Theatre of the Empire of Great Britaine*, adding excellent town plans, battle scenes, and magnificent coats of arms. The next great English map-maker was John Ogilby and, in 1675, he published *Britannia*, Volume I, in which all the roads of England and Wales were engraved on a scale of one inch to the mile, in a massive series of strip maps. From this time onwards, no map was published without roads, and, throughout the eighteenth century, steady progress was made in accuracy, if not always in the beauty of presentation.

The first Ordnance Survey maps came about as a result of Bonnie Prince Charlie's Jacobite rebellion of 1745. It was, however, in 1791, following the successful completion of the military survey of Scotland by General Roy that the Ordnance Survey was formally established. The threat of invasion by Napoleon in the early nineteenth century spurred on the demand for accurate and detailed mapping for military purposes, and, to meet this need, the first Ordnance Survey one-inch map, covering part of Essex, was published in 1805 in a single colour. This was the first numbered sheet in the First Series of one-inch maps.

Over the next seventy years, the one-inch map was extended to cover the whole of Great Britain. Reprints of some of the First Series maps, incorporating various later nineteenth-century amendments, have been published by David & Charles. The reprinted sheets covering most of our area are Numbers 12, 13, 16, and 17. The Ordnance Survey's one-inch maps evolved through a number of 'Series' and 'Editions' to the Seventh Series which was replaced in 1974 by the metric 1:50 000 scale Landranger Series. Between the First Series one-inch and the current Landranger maps, many changes in style, format, content, and purpose have taken place. Colour, for example, first appeared with the timid use of light brown for hill shading on the 1889 one-inch sheets. By 1892, as many as five colours were being used for this scale and, at one stage, the Seventh Series was being printed in no less than ten colours. Recent developments in 'process printing' — a technique in which four basic colours produce any required tint — are now used to produce Ordnance Survey Landranger and other maps series. Through the years, the one-inch Series has gradually turned away from its military origins and has developed to meet a wider user demand. The modern, detailed, full-colour Landranger maps at 1:50 000 scale incorporate Rights of Way and Tourist Information, and are much used for both leisure and business purposes. To compare the old and new approaches to changing demand, see the two map extracts of Bakewell on the following pages.

Modern Ordnance Survey Maps of the Area

The Peak District is covered by Ordnance Survey 1:50 000 scale (1¼ inches to 1 mile) Landranger map sheets 109, 110, 111, 118, 119 and 120. These all-purpose maps are ideal to help you explore the area. Viewpoints, picnic sites, places of interest, caravan and camping sites are shown, as well as public rights of way information such as footpaths and bridleways.

The Peak District is also covered by a single map in the Ordnance Survey Touring Map series at a scale of 1 inch to 1 mile. Guide information on the reverse of this map covers outdoor activities, wildlife, towns and villages as well as three motor tours of interest.

The walker is well catered for by two Ordnance Survey 1:25 000 scale (2½ inches to 1 mile) Outdoor Leisure Maps:

> Sheet 1 — The Peak District - Dark Peak Area
> Sheet 24 — The Peak District - White Peak Area

The areas surrounding these two sheets are also covered at 1:25 000 scale for the walker by the Ordnance Survey Pathfinder series

Motorists will find the Ordnance Survey 1:250 000 scale (1 inch to 4 miles) Routemaster map most useful:

> Sheet 5 — Northern England

An alternative will be found in the form of the Ordnance Survey Motoring Atlas of Great Britain at the larger scale of 1 inch to 3 miles.

To place the area in historical context, the following in the Historical Map and Guide series will be of use: Ancient Britain, Roman Britain, and Britain before the Norman Conquest.

The above maps, and other Ordnance Survey products, are available from most booksellers, stationers and newsagents, or the approved Ordnance Survey stockists below:

Sherratt and Hughes
17 St Ann's Square
Manchester M2 7PD
Tel 061 834 7055

W Hartley Seed
154-160 West Street
Sheffield S1 3ST
0742 722035

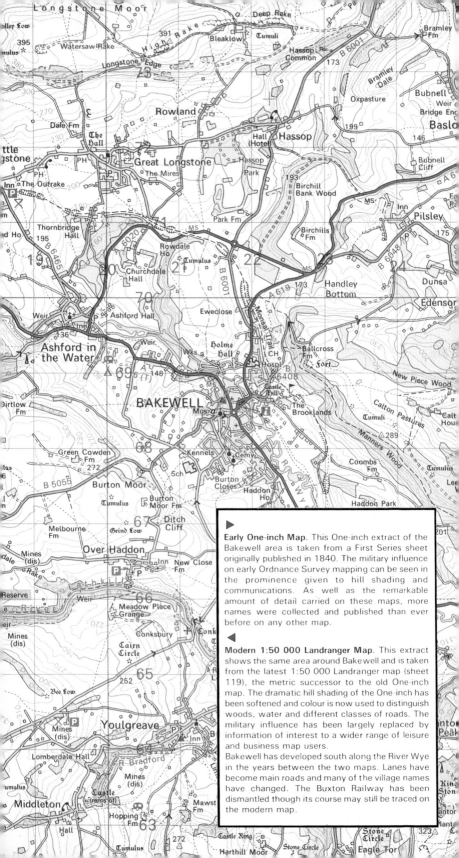

Early One-inch Map. This One-inch extract of the Bakewell area is taken from a First Series sheet originally published in 1840. The military influence on early Ordnance Survey mapping can be seen in the prominence given to hill shading and communications. As well as the remarkable amount of detail carried on these maps, more names were collected and published than ever before on any other map.

Modern 1:50 000 Landranger Map. This extract shows the same area around Bakewell and is taken from the latest 1:50 000 Landranger map (sheet 119), the metric successor to the old One-inch map. The dramatic hill shading of the One-inch has been softened and colour is now used to distinguish woods, water and different classes of roads. The military influence has been largely replaced by information of interest to a wider range of leisure and business map users.

Bakewell has developed south along the River Wye in the years between the two maps. Lanes have become main roads and many of the village names have changed. The Buxton Railway has been dismantled though its course may still be traced on the modern map.

Index

INDEX

INDEX

Selected further reading

Brereton, Peter. *A Touring Guide to English Villages*. 1989. Peerage Books.
Burton, Anthony. *Walking the Line*. 1985. Blandford Press.
Conduit, Brian. *Peak District Walks — Ordnance Survey Pathfinder Guide*. 1989. Ordnance Survey/Jarrold Colour Publications.
Defoe, Daniel. *A Tour through the Whole Island of Great Britain, 1724-6*. 1967. Penguin.
HMSO. *Guide to The Peak District*.
Hoskins, W G. *The Making of the English Landscape*. 1977. Hodder & Stoughton.
Morris, C (ed.). *The Journeys of Celia Fiennes*. 1947. The Cresset Press.
Muir, Richard. *Shell Guide to Reading the Landscape*. 1981. Michael Joseph.
Redhead, Brian. *The National Parks of England and Wales*. 1989. Oxford Illustrated Press.
Room, Adrian. *Pocket Guide to British Place Names*. 1985. Longman.
Spencer, Brian. *More Walks in the Peak District*. 1990. Bartholomew.
Spencer, Brian. *Walk the Peak District*. 1987. Bartholomew.